THE FOUNDATION
OF GODLINESS &
A GODLY LIFE

Happiers Simbo

Preface:

Jesus is real. I say this not because I have read or been lectured to. No! This is through a personal experience and encounter with his life-changing power. My parents, Mr Tapiwa Amos Simbo and Mrs Laiza Simbo, were both preachers in the Methodist church in Zimbabwe, my native country. At a young age they introduced me to Jesus as a savior. They were faithful to the word of God which says, *"Train up a child in the way he should go: and when he is old, he will not depart from it." (Proverbs 22:6).* I am grateful to God for giving me such wonderful parents. At an early age I became a member of the Sunday school. This introduced me to who Jesus is through the reading of the bible and the wonderful, heart-touching Wesleyan songs from the Methodist hymn book. As I grew up and reached the age of accountability I began to pick up a number of errors in the Methodist church which made me fail to differentiate between the real Christian and non-Christian. Although, at some point I became a member of the church choir this exposed me to more anti-Christian behaviours by the church choir members. Consequently whilst at secondary school I began to be involved in drinking, smoking and many other anti-Christian practices which I saw my elder Christian brothers and sisters doing. At last I stopped everything to do with church-going and went deeper into sin. This was a very difficult time of my life as all I was doing was like a fight against my conscience. With my dear friend Langton Mupeta, we could at times sing the songs of God in our state of drunkenness and many times we ended up in tears. It was a real fight against a conscience captivated by the word of God. One Friday evening in September, 1983, I went on a mission to borrow money from my friend Langton. Upon reaching his house I was informed by his neighbours that he was at church. I was surprised and did not know what to do as I desperately needed money that night. Simply for money I decided to go and see him at the church. This was then; the Apostolic Faith Mission of Portland in Zimbabwe which has since divided into several factions. However, I did not intend to go into the church but rather to request him to come out so we could go for drinking. Reaching the church I asked the deacon if my friend was inside and he said he was. I kindly requested to see him but the deacon was unwilling. Upon further request he capitulated, went inside the church and requested my friend to come out. Langton did not have any word to say to me. He just shook my hand and gripped it tight, pulling me into the church. I could not resist as I had a conscience which held the church in high esteem. So I went in and unfortunately they took me right to the front bench. At first I was uneasy because of my attire (work suit) as I was coming from work. The preaching was already in progress. The preacher was speaking in one of the major languages (Ndebele) in Zimbabwe which I did not understand well. Fortunately, he had an interpreter helping him. As I sat there the preacher read a verse of scripture from one of the epistles and said, *"He that committeth sin is of the devil; for the devil sinneth from the beginning. For this purpose the Son of God was manifested, that he might destroy the works of the devil"*, (*1 John 3: 8*). This verse struck at the core of my reason to stop going to church but it also provided me with the cure to this calamity called sin. For the first time I understood that Jesus had come to destroy the works of the devil. As I sat there, half-drunk, I made a vow that I needed to pursue and to understand how Jesus could destroy the devil in me. It took me several visits to the church services to understand what exactly they were preaching about. At last God opened my understanding of what I needed to do. I understood that there was a laid down formula to godliness, not by mankind but from God himself. I came to understand the love with which God had loved me and the entire world all the world through the free underserved gift of his son Jesus Christ and that for our sins he died on the cross. That he became our substitute for death before God. Like the jailer before Paul,

I asked my beloved pastor Finny Gumede what I should do to be saved. He told me of repentance and restitution, justification and sanctification and the baptism of the Holy Ghost, all supported by the word of God which he held so dear. I undertook the task as taught and left all my old ways of living. It was such a dramatic turn around that it surprised my parents, brothers, sisters, relatives and friends. I gathered a lot of books and tools which I had stolen from school and college and personally took them back to the owners. I came to apologize to my parents for the many lies I had told them over the years. This was a task worth taking. As I continued to search myself in the process of repentance God beckoned on me and one day as I prayed alone in the mid of the night, he answered my call for regeneration. Like a flooded river, the grace of God filled my heart. Happiness from within my heart flowed out and I could not help but praise God uncontrollably. This occasion marked a complete turnaround in my life. I became a new creature in Christ. I knew I was born again in spirit.

I, who was speedily becoming a chain smoker and alcohol abuser, instantly became allergic to cigarette smoke and the smell of alcohol. This witnessed to me the power of the salvation of Jesus Christ. All other vices became anathema to my way of life. At the age of twenty-three God saved my soul and up to today, thirty years later, God has not let me down and neither have I wearied to walk with him. I travel by the grace of God, a straight and narrow road, even though the wide road is at my disposal, to the amazement of colleagues, relatives and associates, all because of this wonderful salvation. I am surely built on a sure and invincible foundation which is the Gospel of Christ and the gates of hell cannot confound me. It is all the grace of God. I am so grateful to the Lord Jesus for his mercy. It is my life wish that mankind can by the grace of God know and embrace this foundation which is the Gospel of Christ that they may be saved. The desire to get this message of salvation revived in the world is the reason for the writing of this book. May the Lord God bless all who shall have time to read!

I would like to thank my wife Junior for her unwavering support right from the start of this project. I would also like to express my sincere thank you to her and my daughter Chiedza who read the manuscript and made invaluable corrections and suggestions, without which the book would have been poorer. May God bless them.

Happiers Simbo

Prologue:

Rock of Ages, cleft for me,
Let me hide myself in Thee;
Let the water and the blood,
From Thy riven side which flow'd,
Be of sin the double cure,
Cleanse me from its guilt and power

Not the labor of my hands
Can fulfill Thy law's demands;
Could my zeal no respite know,
Could my tears forever flow,
All for sin could not atone;
Thou must save, and Thou alone.

Nothing in my hand I bring,
Simply to Thy cross I cling;
Naked, come to Thee for dress;
Helpless, look to Thee for grace;
Foul, I to the fountain fly;
Wash me, Savior, or I die.

While I draw this fleeting breath,
When my eyelids close in death,
When I soar through tracts unknown,
See Thee on Thy judgment throne,
Rock of Ages, cleft for me,
Let me hide myself in Thee

By:
Augustus Montague Toplady

INTRODUCTION:

The strength of any building and its ability to withstand the winds, floods and at times even earthquakes depends primarily on the foundation on which it is built. The ability of the building to last for generations depends too on the strength of the foundation on which it is built. In this (21st) century there are buildings in old cities of the world, which are more than a 100 years old and are still intact and, by and large less vulnerable to attacks by the forces of nature than the modern buildings. The buildings have been able to withstand years of torture by the forces of nature because they are built on a strong foundation. Without this strong foundation they would never have managed to stand.

This is the same with the Church of God which this book is all about. For it to withstand the torturous circumstances of the world it needed to be built on a strong foundation. Hence Jesus, giving the analogy of a rock to allude to a strong foundation he would build the church, said to Simon Peter, *"And I say unto thee, That thou art Peter, and upon this Rock I will build my church; and the gates of hell shall not prevail against it" (Matthew 16:18).* By saying upon this rock I will build my church Jesus referred to himself as the rock foundation of the church, not Peter. *"For other foundation can no man lay than that is laid, which is Jesus Christ" (1 Corinthians 3:11).* The church built on the True Foundation called Jesus Christ cannot be confounded by the gates of hell. To be precise, sin in all its forms cannot prevail against that church. If it does then that church is built on another foundation which is not Jesus.

From the beginning of creation it was always God's desire that mankind be like him. God wanted man to be sinless, righteous, holy, and everlasting and to be a ruler as well. Whilst man remained in the Garden of Eden, he eventually succumbed to sin by eating of the forbidden fruit and thereby disobeying God. Man blamed his wife and the serpent for his fall. He forgot that God had instructed him to be the authority to all creation in the Garden of Eden and that the woman was a creation out of him and therefore his responsibility to guide as well. The fall of the woman was through the voice of the snake and the fall of Adam through the voice of the same snake, only by the medium of his wife. Both (Eve and the snake) were supposed to be under Adam's authority. If the King of Eden had refused to succumb to the voice of his wife and the creature, the earth in its shape and form would not have been cursed. Eden would have remained holy and God would have cleansed the world of both Eve and the snake. Unfortunately the king, Adam himself, sinned and in the process defiled the Garden of Eden and consequently the whole world. Once Eden was defiled, God's Spirit could not dwell in an atmosphere of sinfulness. He left and went back heaven. This created a vacuum and a new ruler, Satan came in and took control of world affairs. Without delay thorns and thistles sprung up in the new kingdom of the devil. Sin, hatred, murder, promiscuity, pain and death were immediately planted and nurtured in the former holy garden.

Mankind invariably lost the likeness to God and resembled Satan in all his deeds. They lost the guidance of God and began to be guided by their corrupted conscience which always led them to choose evil over good. Mankind became fleshly and worldly in all their dealings against the statutes of God. Due to their corrupted state, what God condemned as evil became pleasure to them. In that condition mankind condemned itself to spiritual death. Mankind is made up of flesh and the spirit. Whilst the flesh enjoys the pleasures or sins of this world, it will in turn spoil the spirit as well. At the end of this life, the flesh will die and go back to the ground from whence it originated whilst the spirit must go back to God. How was a spoiled spirit going to be received back in heaven, as heaven is a place for the righteous? God made an eternal place of punishment for those who rebel against him and he called it hell. The righteous and Holy God was, however never satisfied with the death of a sinner and their eternal damnation. The Godhead in heaven convened a meeting to plan on how to rescue mankind from the second death, which is the death of the spirit. This rescue plan is called the plan of Salvation. The Christ of God, his only begotten son, volunteered to be the testator of the plan. He had to die a cruel death as a testament is effective after the death of the testator.

This Jesus was to lay a strong foundation on which those built on it would never be confounded by the sins of this world. These sins are the gates of hell, through which mankind will be led to hell. But on this Foundation called Jesus Christ the gates of hell in their entirety would not prevail. Those individuals who are invincible against sin, grouped together are the Church of God.

x

CHAPTER 1

THE FALL OF MANKIND: Genesis 2-3

Scripture informs us that God used to speak directly to Adam in the Garden of Eden. He instructed him to name all creatures and also instructed him on what to eat and what not to eat. After a time God decided to marry Adam to his wife whom Adam named Eve. Eve was created by God from Adam's tissues. She was bone of Adam's bones and tissue of Adam's tissue. Eve received God's instruction through Adam her husband, the recipient of the law of God was Adam and hence the custodian of it. Adam lived in the Garden of Eden with Eve for a time not specified in scripture under the instruction that he had to "…cleave unto his wife…." *(Genesis 2: 24)*. None of the two (husband and wife) was supposed to wander around the garden alone. They had to "cleave" to each other so as not to give occasion to the devil. For a while they obeyed the strict instruction. Satan and his agents kept close watch of Adam and Eve, looking for an opportunity to deceive any one of the two. Satan knew that his best opportunity was with Eve for she only received the instruction of God through Adam. All Satan needed was to introduce doubt into her. He was convinced that if she doubts Adam, she will doubt God. Satan knew this as a precursor to sin and death for the word of God ceases to be living once one doubts it. The word of God is the most powerful weapon and instrument which humankind can ever use only when they have faith in its ability to save and defend. "*For the word of God is quick, and powerful, and sharper than any two edged sword, piercing even to the dividing asunder of soul and spirit, and of the joints and marrow, and is a discerner of the thoughts and intents of the heart*" *(Hebrews 4:12)*. No other known tool can go this deep into the heart of mankind, however its effect is instantly made null and void through unbelief. Satan therefore had to ensure he dragged Eve into the calamity of the unbelieving which leads to alienation by God.

The Serpent and Eve

Satan, at a certain time, had the opportunity to meet with Eve by herself in the garden. Immediately he engaged into a conversation with her, starting with a deceitful question meant to confuse Eve and make her interested in the conversation in an attempt clarify the issue to the devil. The question: *"...yea, hath God said ye shall not eat of every tree of the garden? (Genesis 3: 1b).* The serpent knew that there was only one tree which the inhabitants of the garden were forbidden from eating and hence eating of a single fruit of that tree was breaking the law of God and hence a sin, for *"...sin is the transgression of the law" (1 John 3:4).* He knew that once man sins, he becomes an enemy to God and falls from his grace and favor. Unaware of the plans and aim of the devil Eve willingly engaged into a fatal conversation with the serpent. She tried hard to explain to the serpent what it knew better. The serpent knew how Lucifer the mighty angel had fallen from the grace of God through disobedience to the law. The woman went on to answer the serpent that they were allowed to eat every fruit in the garden with the exception of one. What she did not know was that exception is what the devil wanted her to taste only, never mind to eat. The woman endeavored to explain to the devil what the consequences of eating the forbidden fruit would be *"....ye shall not eat of it, neither shall ye touch it lest ye die" (Genesis 3: 3b).* She even lied to make her answer stronger, for God had never said they should not touch the fruit. Once the serpent saw that the woman had already compromised the truth he straightforwardly and deliberately contradicted the word of God and said, *"...ye shall not surely die".* The woman immediately placed herself in a predicament of who she was going to believe between the serpent and God; she had been taught the statutes of God by Adam and had not heard a direct conversation with God as she was now doing with the serpent. It was therefore easy for Satan to manipulate her. Eve, after the carnal persuasion from the serpent became a convert to the devil. Slowly she began to see imaginary things, *"…that the tree was good for food, and that it was pleasant to the eye, and a tree to be desired to make one wise…" (Genesis 3: 6).* In the absence of Adam she began to doubt all his admonitions about the dangers of disobeying the word of God. Looking at it, it was really a fruit pleasant to the eye but she had to taste it in order know if it was good as a food. Curiously she went on to partake of the fruit in pursuit of false wisdom. It is an irony of sin that it will never appear bad until it has caused total damage. Eve never noticed she was naked neither did Adam see that Eve was naked until he shared the sin with her. Once it was shared, they both realized they were naked. They were stripped of the heavenly garment by the serpent. Satan shifted position away from them and left them to scramble on their own, for why should he worry as if he had forced them to eat; the serpent did not involve himself in the act of plucking off the fruit and eating. All he ensured was that the woman had done it perfectly through continuous encouragement and reassurance. She was also made to believe in the importance of having Adam test the fruit as well and thereafter they would live in a better paradise than Eden. Finally *"…she took the fruit thereof and did eat, and gave also unto her husband with her; and he did eat" (Genesis 3: 6).* They shared willingly the fruit of sin. Having accomplished his mission and knowing the result was death, suffering and nakedness, Satan turned his back and went away to behold their next miserable actions. Immediately Adam and Eve realized they had become naked. No one told them. They saw it and realized it. They were so ashamed and scared that they tried unsuccessfully to hide even from the omnipresent God.

CHAPTER 2

SHADOW OF A COMING MESSIAH

The Nakedness of Sin

Sin is performed in the darkness of the night. Fraud, theft, murder, adultery, fornication are never done openly. However, the result of all this comes as destruction to the perpetrators. The incurable disease called AIDS destroyed a generation in the world, not because it needed to but because it is mainly picked up in the darkness of the night. The adulterers of this world are deceived by the devil that no one will find out that they are fornicators or adulterers. But when AIDS develops and takes root everyone will see and know with no explanation needed. Unfortunately this is usually not before they have spread the disease to the next and most probably innocent person. Women have been the worst victims of this negligence by their promiscuous husbands. It is no surprise that these people still need sympathy when the truth comes out. They take it from Adam and Eve who needed God to sympathize with them after breaking a clear-cut law of the same God.

If Satan fails to use persuasion he goes on to use force. This has always been an option he has used to make people comply with his will. To a non-compromising Christian, homosexuality is an abomination in the same category with murder or adultery. This conclusion is based purely on the bible which is the Christian's charter or covenant and is clearly spelt out in both the old and new testaments, *"Thou shalt not lie with mankind, as with womankind: it is abomination" (Leviticus 18: 22; read 1 Corinthians 6: 9).* To us who believe the Bible to be the word of God and therefore infallible find it difficult to ignore what the scriptures mean here. Something abominable is cursed, diabolical and offensive, according to the modern Oxford dictionary. Jesus came solely to destroy all diabolical activities and practices in the lives of those who would believe in him in order to make them holy and fit for his purpose. *"He that committeth sin is of the devil; for the devil sinneth from the beginning. For this purpose the Son of God was manifested, that he might destroy the works of the devil" (1 John 3: 8).* Jesus never advocated for the destruction of people but their evil works. He died for that. Even today Christians must not compromise with sin, but like their master Jesus, need to stand up and preach for the destruction of any evil in the lives of humankind. It must be emphasized here that like Jesus present day preachers must never advocate for the destruction of sinners, but their sins regardless of what sin it is. It is therefore unfair and wrong in the view of Christians more so in self-declared "Christian govern-ments" for governments to enact laws which force a certain sanctified sin, in their opinion, to be accepted of all people and religions. It cannot be right to coerce Christians through legal instruments to trash their values and accept this anti-bible behavior as a human right. That is a blatant violation of the Christian's right and an attempt to rewrite the bible. As a Christian I have no doubt that anyone who claims to be a Christian whilst entertaining sins has left the faith and become an anti-Christ. This is far from being judgmental, for the scriptures are the judge and we follow scriptures, not human adventures.

God created a man and a woman for two reasons. First to love each other and be partners in life through marriage and secondly whilst they live together to procreate. Yes, they may fail to reproduce children due to barrenness but again that will be the will of God to a very small minority. Some (a minority again) may choose to opt out of child bearing. However, to have a man who does not love a woman to still want to have children by using money to sponsor the same woman to have an embryo implanted into her is a first-class abomination. It is an abuse of the womanhood and a violation of their rights by being used as surrogates for the sake of money. Furthermore it is a child's right to have a mother and a father. But this birthright is trashed in order to uphold the human enacted rights of two selfish individuals acting against nature to gratify their misplaced appetites. I have no hatred for gay people but like prostitutes and drunkards they cannot be accepted as Christians unless they repent and leave their abhorrent sin of not only violating God's plan but also the rights of women, children and the Christian society *(Galatians 5: 19; Leviticus 18:22).*

Adam the Fugitive

"*And the eyes of them both were opened, and they knew that they were naked; and they sewed fig leaves together, and made themselves aprons. And they heard the voice of the Lord God walking in the garden in the cool of the day: and Adam and his wife hid themselves from the presence of the Lord God amongst the trees of the garden" (Genesis 3: 7-8)*

It was God's system to come at the cool of each day to meet with Adam in the Garden of Eden. On the day of Adam's fall God still paid him a visit although he knew that Adam had fallen. As he approached their meeting place Adam and Eve his wife were nowhere to be seen. They had vanished into the bushes of Eden in an attempt to hide away from their omnipresent creator. With the love of a father who has lost a son, God called Adam and said, "*Adam, where art thou?*" The voice was so strong and ringing right in his ear that he could not help but to answer from the bushes where he was hiding. This was now a different Adam who had become a stranger to the truth. His answer to God was to blame his wife and to lie. What he forgot was the wife did not sin for him; he received sin with his own hand. The wife blamed the serpent. So Adam and Eve tried to maintain their innocence even though they had become sinners. But God knew they were both at fault and that they needed to be punished first and then to be rescued. Many things changed immediately as a result of the fall of Adam. The Garden of Eden lost its state of a paradise. Thorns and thistles grew as a sign of permanent pain on the earth starting in the Garden of Eden. Adam became a labourer and Eve a child bearer but in pain. Hatred and murder emerged and in no time Cain murdered his own brother Abel, becoming the first murderer ever known. King Adam lost his royalty to animals and became meat to some of them until today with other small insects biting him and his posterity seasonally and at will *"Thou madest him to have dominion over the works of thy hands; thou hast put all things under his feet" (Psalm 8)*. Creatures have declared war against the posterity of Adam. Budgets are set aside to fight insects like flies and mosquitoes with mankind sometimes losing the battle. Human mortality rates can never be controlled without controlling the proliferation of these enemies of mankind. It became a world of pain, tears and death and indeed it shall remain so until God at his own time decides to restore the conditions of the Garden of Eden. At that time death shall also be vanquished and humankind will again live eternally.

The Messiah Promised

"And I will put enmity between thee and the woman, and between thy seed and her seed; it shall bruise thy head, and thou shalt bruise his heel". (Genesis 3:15)

The desire of the Godhead right from the beginning was for mankind to be a true resemblance of their image. This plan faltered because of sin. Sin is one characteristic that God will never be associated with except in its eradication. God loved the man and woman he created in his image. He hated the sin they had acquired but retained the love for them. Because he loved them he set out to eradicate that which he hated in mankind: sin!

Immediately after the sinful encounter between the

woman and the serpent, God proclaimed a perpetual warfare between the two. This warfare was expanded to include the whole kingdom of God and that of the devil. No wonder since then until the end of time there shall continue to be a fierce war between good and evil and wickedness and righteousness in the world. There is conflict between good and evil in the very hearts of mankind. These are the fruits of the fall of Adam and Eve from grace. The fall itself was a consequence of the unity in wickedness between Eve and the serpent. Unity in wickedness is always a danger to the emissaries, short lived and always ends in a calamity. In this whole scenario between Eve and the serpent the major player was Satan himself with the serpent being his faithful agent. Therefore the curse as it were seemed directed at the serpent yet in reality it was directed at the father of all lies and deceit, Satan himself. He persuaded Eve to eat that she was not supposed to eat and God made him (Satan) to eat that he did not want to eat (dust). Never again was he going to be next to the throne of God, but to descend further into the bottomless pit at an appointed time. "How art thou fallen O Lucifer."

After partaking of sin, Adam and Eve entered the darkest hour of their lives. They had no God. Whilst they were in that situation, the loving and Almighty God remembered them. He promised them about the coming "seed of the woman" *(Genesis 3:15)*. The sure promise of the Messiah. The product of the woman, a virgin, with no man involved in its conception was to bruise the head of the serpent. He was to bruise the head of the serpent and vanquish his power and overthrow his kingdom by his death on the cross of Calvary. He was to shed that precious blood to cleanse the spoiled and conflict ridden hearts of mankind. During the conflict Satan would fight and in turn bruise the heel of the woman so as to try and stop the plan of Salvation. All the conflicts endured by the Lord Jesus Christ from childhood to Gethsemane, the rejection by Peter, the desertion by the disciples, the prosecution and condemnation by Pilate and the scourging, the vinegar and lastly the piercing spear were a bruise to the heel of the seed of the woman as per the prophecy. The climax of that bruise was the nailing of the Lord to the cross. Rough, barbaric and merciless was the act that even God could not endure the sight of it and he left Jesus alone to go through the agony and Satan's brutality carried out through the hand of mankind *(Matthew 27:46).* This was a joyful moment to the devil and his associates; little did they realise that this final bruise to the seed of a virgin was to be the fatal blow to his (Satan's) kingdom for the scripture say, *"For as much then as the children are partakers of flesh and blood he also himself likewise took part of the same; that through death he may destroy him that had the power of death, that is the devil, (Hebrews 2: 14).* The messiah had to test the very weapon with which the devil had used to sink nations by going into it to see if it had power to sink him too. Whilst in death he challenged it and it left him and by it he destroyed the very master of death, the devil.

The Pre-Foundation:

After the fall God sent mankind out of Eden with a blessing to be fruitful and to multiply and replenish the earth. Though they had become sinful Adam and Eve went out with the blessing and did as per instruction from God. Nations and kindred descended out of them. All these nations, kindred and tongues had all inherited sin from Adam and Eve and none of them worshiped or feared God. They were deeply in sin and needed some means to rescue them. But to rescue man from sin the Messiah or Savior also needed a fleshly body to offer as a sacrifice *"Wherefore when he cometh into the world, he saith, Sacrifice and offering thou wouldest not, but a body hast thou prepared me" (Hebrews 10: 5).* To prepare the body God called a man out of the nations through whom a new nation founded on the godly characteristics of sacrifice,

9

obedience, trust and faith would be born. Through that nation would God incarnate come through to be a propitiation for the sin of fallen mankind?

The Call of Abram:

The call of Abram was composed of an injunction or decree followed by a promise. The injunction or decree would lead to the promise. Failure to match up to the decree would mean failure to get the promise. Abram did not know God as he was an offspring of an idolatrous man, Terah. Terah was living among a tribe of idol worshipers and Abram was a partaker of the same kind of worship. He had done nothing to please God as he was a true descendent of fallen Adam.

However, the omnipotent God who alone is able to know the secrets and intensions of the hearts of humankind searched among the nations and tribes of the earth and found old Abram and his equally old wife, Sarah. They had nothing special except that the imaginations of their hearts were inclined to the will of God. The power of predestination followed Abram in his sorry circumstances of sin, for the call was upon him to fulfill the will of God.

The Injunction:

"Now the Lord had said unto Abram, get thee out of thy country, and from thy kindred, and from thy father's house, unto a land that I will shew thee:" (Genesis 12:1).

Abram was commanded to leave all things that are dearest to all of us. Was he really going to willingly leave all friends and relatives and the very land of nativity to follow a God he had not seen? He was an owner of lands and beasts of different kinds. Was he going to abandon these for a land he was going to be shown only, for the Bible never said he will be given the land, but simply says, "unto a land that I will shew thee"? God wanted Abram to come

10

out of all these associations in a show of trust in God who gave the decree. Abram was to go alone with his wife Sara to meet the wild beasts of the wilderness and all the barbarous nations littering the way to Canaan. His trust was to be in God who called him and that he alone was able to lead him to Canaan, the land of strangers.

A Blessing to Nations:

"I will make thee a great nation, and I will bless thee, and make thy name great, and thou shalt be a blessing: And I will bless them that bless thee, and curse him that curseth thee: and in thee shall all families of the earth be blessed" *(Genesis 12: 2, 3).*

God's aim in persuading Abram to leave his native land was not to make him rich. It was the beginning of the laying of a strong, flawless and everlasting foundation for the rescue of all the descendants of Adam from the clutches of sin. All humankind descends from Adam are by virtue of their nature born sinful without exception. Therefore the promise which says, "and in thee shall all the families of the earth be blessed" means that the blessing was to be universal. The Lord Jesus who is the fulfilment of this promise said in confirmation of the universality of the promise said, *"For God so loved the world that he gave his only begotten son, that whosoever believeth in him should not perish, but have everlasting life"* *(John 3:16).* Abram's faithful and unconditional acceptance of the promise therefore struck a death blow to the devil.

Abram in response to the call left the homeland to see the land God promised to show him. It was the land of Canaan. In due course God followed up on his promise and Sarah, Abram's aged wife, gave birth to a boy whom they called Isaac according to God's instruction that they should name him so. With Isaac, God wanted to establish an everlasting covenant. Isaac was a child born of an old couple that had gone past their reproductive age. He was a product of the faith of Abram in the omnipotent God. The bible says Abram believed God that he would be a father of many nations and it was counted to him for righteousness. The covenant which God made with Abraham was to culminate in the birth of the seed of a woman promised in Genesis. This seed of a woman (Jesus) was also to be a product of faith in God and born out of the purity of virginity. Without God's direct intervention Isaac could not have born, as Sarah was forty years past her reproductive years, and likewise without God's direct intervention Jesus would not have been born for it is impossible for a virgin to have a child without the involvement of a man. But God the creator planted the seed in the womb of Mary the mother of Jesus to fulfil the prophecy which said the serpent or Satan's head will be bruised by the seed of a woman without the involvement of a man. The seed of a woman was born of the lineage of Isaac in the flesh. The promise to Abraham that nations will be blessed through him was fulfilled in the birth of Jesus Christ who destroyed the veil of separation between the Jew and the gentile, *"that whosoever believeth in him should not perish but have everlasting life" (John 3:16).*

CHAPTER 3

THE FOUNDATION

The Pronouncements:

"For she shall bring forth a son, and thou shall call his name JESUS: for he shall save his people from their sins" *(Matthew 1:21)*

Our Lord Jesus Christ was born on this earth for a purpose to save mankind from both their committed and imputed sins. This Jesus, as we have seen already, was to be a product of a woman without any involvement of a man. His was a purposeful birth with its aim to eradicate his people's sins. That was the purpose of his journey to earth.

Indeed, after this first angelic announcement Mary conceived of the Holy Ghost for the angel said to her in the second announcement:

"And the angel answered and said unto her, the Holy Ghost shall come upon thee and the power of the Highest shall overshadow thee: therefore that holy thing which shall be born of thee shall be called the son of God" *(Luke 1:35)*

and nine months later Jesus was born at Bethlehem of Judah. Although he was God incarnate he lived an ordinary man's life being subject to his mother and to Joseph Mary's husband for 30 years. He demonstrated expected humbleness children should have to their parents both in childhood and as adults, for he came not to destroy but to fulfill the law. The law which God had given to Moses emphasized the importance of respect for parents and Jesus followed this to the book, setting an example for his followers.

When the time to commence his mission on Earth was up he went to Jordan to be baptized of John, his forerunner. Soon after he was baptized a third announcement came from God saying, *"Thou art my beloved son; in thee I am well pleased" (Luke 3: 22).* Jesus went into the wilderness and spent forty days and forty nights being tempted of the devil and above all he prayed and fasted. He subdued the devil through a myriad of temptations.

He came back into Galilee to make a fourth announcement which sealed the beginning of the Gospel of the Kingdom of God. *"Now after that John was put in prison, Jesus came into Galilee, preaching the Gospel of the Kingdom of God, And saying, The time is fulfilled, the Kingdom of God is at hand: repent ye and believe the gospel" (Mark 1: 14-15).* In the meantime many people who had listened to the preaching of John the Baptist had learnt about repentance. They had repented and turned away from their sins but now the announcement said they must believe so that the power of God may build a kingdom within their hearts. Many of the disciples of Jesus including Peter, Andrew, John and James had heard the doctrine of repentance from John the Baptist. Immediately at the call of Jesus to believe they did and they were saved from their sins. They separated themselves from all worldliness and sin in response to the call for repentance and dropped down earthly tasks and business and followed Jesus. Like Abraham they departed and left relatives and friends to follow Jesus the stranger of Galilee.

The Exposure:

When Jesus came into the coasts of Caesarea Philippi, he asked his disciples, saying, Whom do men say that I the Son of man am? And they said, Some say that thou art John the Baptist: some, Elias; and others, Jeremias, or one of the prophets. He saith unto them, But whom say ye that I am? And Simon Peter answered and said, Thou art the Christ, the Son of the living God. (Matthew 16: 13-16)

Jesus selected his twelve apostles from those who heard the preaching of the Gospel, repented, believed and were saved. He gave them the power of the Holy Ghost to become the children of God. Whilst he was with them he performed many miracles and with the admission of both his admirers and enemies alike his teaching was found to be strong, unique and convincing. He was the great talk of the nation from Galilee to Judea and beyond. At some point after having been with his disciples for some time, Jesus took the opportunity to find out if his disciples and the generality of people understood who he was. This was important to him as his disciples were the very people who were to remain on Earth preaching and spreading the gospel.

Firstly he wanted to know from his apostles what the ordinary man and woman perceived him to be. Though he was a member of the triune God, Jesus whilst on earth referred to himself as a son of man. This was his great lesson of humility to his disciples first and all his followers. Jesus preferred his works to speak and witness for him than titles and names. That is why his mission on earth was filled with all manner of good works on those he had an encounter with. To the people of Israel anyone who performed wonders was a prophet and nothing more than that. To them the messiah was to redeem them from the bondage of the Romans. This Jesus, ready to redeem all of them from the bondage of sin and disease was just but a prophet. By so doing they missed the point although they had been with him for thirty-three years.

That he was just a prophet was obviously a wrong answer so Jesus turned to his disciples and paused a like question now directly to them: *"but whom say ye that I am?"* It was a moment of deep thought for the disciples who had so much influence from both common people and also from the leaders of the people. The leaders of the people (Pharisees and Sadducees), through jealousy, fear,

15

prejudice and simple hatred were out to undermine Jesus's humble but heavenly work. He had just warned them about the leaven of the Pharisees and Sadducees. It is understandable some could still be in a state of confusion and Jesus aimed to clear this from their hearts and minds as well. The Holy Spirit, who is the teacher and counselor descended on Peter and there he went on to answer the Lord's question and said *"Thou art the Christ, the Son of the living God".* Peter clearly demonstrated his knowledge of Jesus Christ not as the son of man but of God. He had managed to differentiate Jesus from other prophets including John the Baptist who had previously preached the doctrine of repentance to him. He realized that whilst all prophets had preached the word of God but none had touched anything about the salvation of the soul. Immediately and with joy Jesus pronounced a blessing to Peter and that God had on behalf of the other disciples revealed it to him through his own mercy. Peter had no reason to feel or act better than others but to be like his master and humbly acknowledge God's providence. His best gift was to know that he was blessed for those pronounced by God to be blessed are blessed indeed. Finally, Jesus had exposed himself to his disciples through the mouth of one of his disciples so all his disciples would henceforth never call him the son of man but the son of the living God.

The Sure Refuge:

"Therefore thus saith the Lord GOD, Behold, I lay in Zion for a foundation a stone, a tried stone, a precious corner stone, a sure foundation: he that believeth shall not make haste. Judgment also will I lay to the line, and righteous-ness to the plummet: and the hail shall sweep away the refuge of lies, and the waters shall overflow the hiding place. And your covenant with death shall be disannulled, and your agreement with hell shall not stand; when the overflowing scourge shall pass through, then ye shall be

trodden down by it" (Isaiah 28: 16-18)

Whilst mankind through the deception of sin seeks to find refuge and happiness in vain things like money, education, power and many other fantasies, God through his own mercy and with full knowledge of the vanity of these things sought to find them a true everlasting refuge and happiness. This refuge was to be based on Abraham's type of faith. The Abraham faith is based on a solid foundation of sacrifice, obedience and separation. The word of God states that all people have sinned and fall short of the glory of God. Therefore, unless one is anchored on the true foundation they remain sinful. It is only when one anchors oneself on the true foundation that the false refuge is swept away. Righteousness and holiness becomes the emblem and insignia of men and women built on this foundation as lies and deception are swept away. This will bring to naught the covenants with death and hell which the world of sin so much cherishes. There will be a new covenant of faith in God, which propelled Abraham to depart from his native and idolatrous country and people to an unknown land. He was to be father of a new nation and people. The people of all nations who would accept this Abraham like faith in God would likewise separate themselves from all sin in order to be built on the sure and secure foundation. They will find refuge and solace in the God of heaven. The foundational stone is a precious, tried and tested one and is named Jesus. Those who will be built on it shall embrace the grace through faith in Jesus. The world as it were with all its temptations and tribulations will not in any way confound them, not of their own ability but due to the strength of the foundation upon which they are built. However, many in the world will stumble at the stone as they view it not as a cave of refuge but rather a rock of offence, since it will expose and rebuke their carnal excesses on earth.

Jesus the Rock of Ages:

"And Jesus answered and said unto him, Blessed art thou, Simon Barjona: for flesh and blood hath not revealed it unto thee, but my Father which is in heaven. And I say also unto thee, That thou art Peter, and upon this rock I will build my church; and the gates of hell shall not prevail against it". (Matthew 16: 17-18).

After all prophesies and pronouncements, time came when Jesus had to reveal himself as the rock foundation of salvation to the world, beginning with his disciples. His question to his disciples was meant just for that particular purpose. Peter under the influence of the Holy Ghost answered the question of Jesus correctly that he was the son of the living God. What was the Son of God on Earth and in flesh to do? He was here to lay a foundation upon which the church of God was to be built on earth. He was tried by all means possible. He was injured, bruised, hated and persecuted to make him recant his mission for the salvation of mankind but he stood firm. He was crushed but never broken until he died shedding his precious and undefiled blood for the remission of sins. All the breaking up of his body and shedding of blood was to provide brick and mortar for God to build a foundation for his church to be built upon.

Peter's answer to Jesus was that *"You are the Christ"* and Jesus confirmed and reinforced this truth of his being the Christ of God and the Rock foundation upon which the church of God was to be built. He was the author and finisher of the Christian faith by his birth, suffering, death and resurrection. Through his obedience to suffer and die the death of the cross he wrote our salvation. Through his death and resurrection he built a strong and unbreakable foundation to draw souls of men and women to him, unite them to make a church that they may rest and forever depend on him. The knowledge that Jesus is the Christ and the practical faith in that knowledge is the foundation upon which true, lasting Christianity is built in an individual. Without this knowledge, faith and practice, Christianity becomes a mere religion.

The Gates of Hell which are the sins of this world cannot prevail against one built on this foundation, because once on this foundation one is given power of the Holy Ghost to become the son or daughter of God regardless of denominational affiliations. They are adopted into the family of God to become brothers and sisters to Christ. They can no longer sin because they are born of God. This spiritual birth is the second birth which supersedes the first with its failures. Their spiritual man is now able to suppress the wishes of the carnal man. It is simply an error to declare that there is no one righteous on earth that is to make the cross of Christ of no effect. It is whilst we live upon this earth that men and women are made righteous. If there are professors of Christ who are also busy bodies in sin, it is because they have never seen or known his power.

The Apostles:

"And I will give unto thee the keys of the kingdom of heaven: and whatsoever thou shalt bind on earth shall be bound in heaven: and whatsoever thou shalt loose on earth shall be loosed in heaven". (Matthew 16: 19)

Peter who was one of the apostles of Jesus was blessed to have given a clear understanding of who the Lord Jesus was: not a son of man but the Christ of God. Jesus Christ confirmed the fundamental truth that his aim was to build a Church on Earth which would be invincible against sin and worldliness. This church was going to be a kingdom within the kingdoms of the world. However, for now it would appear to be subject to the kingdoms of this world concerning world governance. In terms of spiritual governance the church was to be led and indeed governed according to the statutes and laws of the kingdom of heaven to which it actually belongs. Jesus the founder and foundation of the church was within a few days going to be made a sacrifice to seal the foundation of the church by his blood and there after rise from the dead and be taken to heaven. He knew that he needed builders to remain building upon the laid foundation, to feed the church and govern it. Turning to Peter and him representing the other disciples he said, *"I will give unto thee, the keys of the Kingdom of heaven: and whatsoever thou shalt bind on earth shalt be bound in heaven: and whatsoever thou shalt loose on earth shalt be loosed in heaven".* So the keys to preach the gospel, heal and cast out devils were conferred to Peter and his colleagues. They were to lead and guide the church of Christ according to the rules of the Gospel. They were to be faithful and exemplary to the flock of God and the world at large. This was and is still important in order for the members of the church of God to follow and the generality of the people to be converted to Christ. The apostles were and are still required to demonstrate that they are built upon an immovable foundation Christ, through their holy conduct and conversation. They should never compromise a little to the world. In so doing they would become in turn a sure foundation upon the foundation which is Christ. They are the founding example of the practicality of the Gospel of Christ on which they are themselves built, in order to spread it to the gentiles and the Jews together. So the word says, *"You are built upon the foundation of the apostles and prophets, Jesus Christ being the chief corner stone" (Ephesians 2:20).* Yes, Jesus the chief cornerstone or the base foundation, for whenever the apostles build they will need Jesus Christ to strengthen and knit the members together into a holy church fit for the habitation of the Holy Ghost.

In turn the word of God from the faithful and holy ministers was to be realized, even today not as the word of man but of God and received accordingly by the church. The church being convinced that the ministers are messengers of God for the spreading of his good news to the world.

The Holy Communion between the ministers and the church is a prerequisite for the effective and unhindered spreading of the Gospel of Christ.

CHAPTER 4

LAYING THE FOUNDATION-THE PASSION

Shadow to Reality:

"And as they were eating, Jesus took bread, and blessed it, and brake it, and gave it to the disciples, and said, Take, eat; this is my body. And he took the cup, and gave thanks, and gave it to them, saying, Drink ye all of it; For this is my blood of the new testament, which is shed for many for the remission of sins. But I say unto you, I will not drink henceforth of this fruit of the vine, until that day when I drink it new with you in my Father's kingdom". (Matthew 26:26-29)

The Passover was instituted by God for the children of Israel in Egypt. At the first Passover they were asked by Moses to slaughter a lamb per household and eat it all *(Exodus 12:1-10)*. When they followed the statutes of the Passover as instructed by Moses, the Israelites were redeemed from the bondage of Pharaoh, the king of Egypt. Since then God instructed them to celebrate the Passover every year. Jesus said he never came to destroy the law but to fulfil it. After the thirty-three and half years on Earth, time came for Jesus to be sacrificed as the true Paschal lamb. The Lord Jesus Christ knew that that particular Passover was his last on earth. He therefore took occasion to teach and instruct his apostles the meaning and symbols of his death as related to the ceremonial Passover. He knew that during this particular Passover, type will be changed to anti-type and shadows will be changed to reality. The true meaning of the Passover which began in Egypt was at this time going to be fulfilled. Having gathered all of his twelve apostles including the traitor he took unleavened bread as per the law of the ceremony, broke and blessed it and took a jar of wine, gave thanks to Mighty God and he gave them to eat and drink. Since the introduction of the Passover in Egypt, there was an annual shedding of blood of animals and breaking of their bodies. These bodies were supposed to be consumed to completion during the feast. But Jesus, as he replaced the shadow of things with reality he removed the former types and replaced them with symbols, as the real blood was about to be shed and the true body to be broken once and for all. Going forward, no more blood was to be shed for redemption as that of Jesus would last through eternity and no more body was to be broken for his body was broken for all ages. Henceforth the Passover ceremony was going to be symbolic and a remembrance of the great sacrifice for the sins of mankind by God who sacrificed his own son to redeem mankind from the clutches of sinfulness. No more was it for the remembrance of the Israeli departure from Egypt as the body and blood of Jesus is for universal redemption of mankind, not a particular nation. His blood which was to be shed once was to do away with the old covenant based on the blood of animals to a new covenant based on the pure and undefiled blood of the son of God. Whereas the blood of animals was to remove man from human suppression, the blood of Jesus was to remove them from the suppression of sin. This blood is the emblem of the New Testament. As the blood of animals meant exoneration from death in Egypt, the blood of Jesus means exoneration from eternal death of the soul.

The Lamb without blemish:

"This is my beloved Son, in whom I am well pleased" *(Matthew 3:17)*

At its inception by God in Egypt the Passover had specific instruction that needed to be followed for it to be effective in its purpose. The lamb was to be without blemish, a one-year-old male sheep or goat. This lamb was supposed be a shadow of the purity of Jesus, which it symbolized. It is reasonable to assume that it took the children of Israel a difficult time for close to six hundred thousand families to find such a pure lamb for each household. No doubt the search needed diligent and persistent searching. However, any one family which wanted to go out of Egypt had no choice but to find a lamb without blemish, regardless of how hard or difficult it was. Jesus Christ being the fulfillment of these types, the chief corner stone and the rock foundation of the Gospel of God was meant to be a true and unblemished Lamb of God. True to expectation, Jesus's purity was witnessed by God, prophets, angels, friends, enemies and foes alike. He was a real lamb without blemish. God at the transfiguration witnessed Jesus as his beloved son in whom he was pleased. God is pleased of nothing but purity. All prophets from Moses to John the Baptist spoke of Jesus' uprightness and holiness and the angel said *"That holy thing which shall be born of thee shall be called the Son of God" (Luke 1:35).* His enemies and foes attempted to soil him as a malefactor and devil. They called him evil names like Beelzebub *(Mark 3:22)* to gratify their hatred of him until they managed to convince and convert the nation of Israel to be against the King of glory. Having achieved this, the populace was made ready to slaughter the true Paschal Lamb unawares. Starting with the traitor disciple Judas Iscariot, he had nothing evil to witness to the scribes and elders about Jesus. He saw their desire to kill him and in that ego he discovered an opportunity to get some money. With this apparent opportunity and knowing the power and divinity of Jesus, he was convinced he would get money and Jesus would escape for he had seen them wanting to kill him many times and he had escaped. Judas' mistake was twofold. He chose not to believe Jesus, who had told them on several occasions that he was heading to Jerusalem to be killed by the hands of sinners. Secondly, his love for money had become a snare to him as it was out of control.

At last when all was done and the lamb was being roasted and condemned to be slaughtered Judas realized his mistake, took the money, went back to his companions in sin and testified, *"saying I have sinned in that I have betrayed innocent blood" (Matthew 27:4),* again proving Jesus to be a lamb without blemish. The Jews took Jesus from the high priest to Pilate, so he could pass the final death sentence. Pilate, a gentile judge, saw that Jesus was innocent and that out of envy they wanted to kill him. As if that was not enough his wife sent a message to him saying, *"have nothing to do with that just man..............."* *(Matthew 27:19).* This was another gentile witness to the fact that JESUS was a lamb without blemish. The Jewish rulers called several witnesses to testify against Jesus as required by the Law of Moses but they all failed to agree making their witness non-binding. Jesus the Lamb of God had to be sacrificed so as to shed blood for the remission of sins. Though sinless and with no human witness able to condemn him as a malefactor a way had to be found and only his own testimony would condemn him. The Spirit of God moved the high priest to ask Jesus if was the son of God upon which Jesus answered, *"thou hast said"* *(Matthew 26: 64)* and that became enough to condemn him for blasphemy yet it was true that he was the son of God. The high priest rent his clothes and said no more witness was needed but to go ahead with the crucifixion as he realized that no witness was ever going to come forth. His confession of truth was sin to his enemies. He had to die but with a clear witness of being sinless. As he gave up the ghost and his Spirit committed to God many signs and wonders occurred and looking at him the Roman soldier said, *"truly he was the son of God."* Jesus therefore became a true fulfilment of the lamb slaughtered in Egypt to redeem Israel. He was slaughtered in innocence to lay a strong foundation for the remission of human sinfulness.

Death the Old Covenant:

"A new covenant, he hath made the first old. Now that which decayeth and waxed old is ready to vanish away" (Hebrews 8: 13)

As Jesus approached the crucifixion in order to lay the foundation for Christianity, he spoke of a new covenant and the death of the old. His blood was to be the guarantor of the new covenant or testament and was ready to be shed. At and during the same process of laying the foundation of the new covenant the first had to be torn apart and be made old and of no effect. Both processes would happen simultaneous as the old give way to the new. That which decays had to give way to the everlasting. The fleshly covenant based on the law was to give way to the covenant of grace. Whilst God incarnate was being made the sacrifice and lamb for the slaughter, the scribes and elders were being made the tools to destroy that which they were supposed to enforce, which is the Law of Moses. The scribes and elders of Israel were the principal teachers and rulers of the Jewish religion and nation. They were the custodians of the old covenant as given to Moses at Sinai. God looked upon them for its observance and enforcement. In the old covenant were divine laws from God which, if followed, would make mankind holy before God. However, because the law was external and had no control of the human conscience it was for the flesh to try and abide by the law. This proved impossible as mankind failed to do the will of God even though the desire to do so was in them. Hence God decided to lay a new foundation through which the human conscience would be controlled and led to do right.

The high priest (Caiaphas), together with the scribes and elders of Israel being the leaders of the Jewish religion and nation, engineered the death of an innocent man through lies, hypocrisy, and deceit. They moved the nation to tell lies and partake in the shedding of innocent blood. It was in the courtyard of the high priest where the Lord Jesus was more abused than anywhere else during his passion. Instead of the high priest' home being a refuge for the oppressed and suffering it became the headquarters for humiliation, inflicting pain and spilling of innocent blood. The law for which they stood for was in conflict with their behavior. The law said the Sabbath was holy but in their zeal to see the death of Jesus Christ the Jewish leaders tasked the guards to work on a Sabbath and ensure the Lord's grave was concreted and secured that he would not come out or be, according to them stolen by the disciples *(Matthew 27:62-64)*. The destruction of Sabbath observance and other laws was therefore done at the pinnacle of the Jewish religion. By this act God wanted to ensure that the Old Testament gave way to the new as the foundation was being laid.

The Passion:

"If the ox shall push a manservant or a maidservant; he shall give unto their master thirty shekels of silver, and the ox shall be stoned" (Exodus 21:32)

The Passion of Christ is that last journey of his life which includes his arrest, trial, suffering, crucifixion, burial and resurrection from the dead. The passion of Jesus Christ therefore began in the garden of Gethsemane. Soon after his last supper with the disciples he went to pray the whole night in the garden. He was accompanied to the garden by his three disciples Peter, James and John. Unfortunately they were all tired and sleeping throughout that night. Jesus knew what he was facing; he knew the total contents of the sacrifice. The scourging, beatings, spiting, the abusive language, the desertion by his disciples, the treachery of Judas, the denials by Peter, all the human abuse and lastly the crucifixion were visible to his divine eye and knowledge, for these were all brick and mortar for the building of the foundation of the Church. The situation he was in was fertile ground for the temptation of the devil, so Jesus had to pray to God for strength through the tribulations. Jesus carried a human body which was subject to pain and having lived in flesh for over thirty years he was acquainted with what pain can do. He was aware that the phase he was entering was that of extraordinary pain, which has never been experience neither will ever be experienced by a living being. He passionately prayed until blood veins gave in and sweat came out mixed with blood. God through his grace strengthened him through the sacrificial suffering.

As Jesus prayed in the garden, Judas, one of his disciples was busy in the courts of the enemy planning for his master's death. He wanted a price for the work of deception he was about to undertake. Finally they settled for a price of thirty pieces of silver, which was the price for a slave. This was paid immediately, well in advance of the work being carried out to ensure no reversal by the seller.

After prayer, Jesus with his three disciples walked out of the garden and met the rest of the disciples where they had left them. Judas Iscariot, who was leading a gang of Jews and gentiles eager to apprehend Jesus, immediately arrived and kissed him in order for him to be identified from his companions. Convinced that this was their prey, the abuse started and continued that night until they nailed him to the cross the following morning. He was taken to the high priest where witnesses were lined up but failed to agree in their accusations. Peter denied both knowledge and relationship to Jesus as he sat at the high priest's house. Judas, realising his mistake proceeded to hang himself. Jesus was taken to Pilate who reluctantly, and out of failure for principle and justice, could not judge properly. He wanted to save his position and to make people happy rather than to stick to the principle of justice. Pilate tried to trade Jesus with Barabbas but the masses chose Barabbas to live and Jesus to die for that is what he came for to save sinners from death not for sinners to die in his place. Pilate himself went ahead to scourge Jesus, becoming the first man to lawfully condemn Jesus to death knowing that he was innocent. Said Pilate when the Jews cried for Jesus to be crucified *"......Why what evil hath he done?" (Matthew 27:23).* He found no fault in him but still went ahead to condemn Jesus sealing the condemnation with a scourge. As he suffered he brought bitter enemies together the Roman guards and the officers of the high priest. They were partners in mocking and in inflicting maximum pain on him. As they walked him out of the city to crucify him, God's providence brought a gentile disciple from Africa who was forced by the Roman and Jewish murderers to assist the Lord to carry the cross through the last mile of the journey as they dragged him to be crucified out of the city at Calvary' cross. He became a partaker of the sufferings of Christ. Reaching Golgotha, they nailed the innocent saviour to the cross. With sheer determination to make his death as bitter, sour and painful they during the last moments of his life gave him vinegar mixed with gall where many dying would have been given wine. Against the wishes of his enemies at last a bold inscription was put on his cross, *"Jesus, King of the Jews".* Although the Jews protested against this statement, Pilate refuted them and ignored their request to remove it.

Witnesses to the truth of the Resurrection:

"Who was delivered for our offences, and was raised again for our justification" (Romans 4:25).

The making of the foundation upon which the Church of God would subsequently be built was going to be incomplete and of no consequence without the resurrection of Jesus from the dead. He had to conquer the cruelty of sin by being nailed to the cross to shed blood and rose from the dead for the justification of sinners and subjugation of death and the grave. So the resurrection of Christ was part of the process in the plan of salvation. His resurrection had many witnesses to it including the angels, Jewish guards, his disciples and apostles.

An Angel's Testimony:

"And the angel answered and said unto the women, Fear not ye: for I know that ye seek Jesus, which was crucified. He is not here: for he is risen, as he said. Come, see the place where the Lord lay". (Matthew 28: 5, 6).

Early on Passover Sunday of the passion of Jesus Christ, two women disciples of Jesus Christ were determined to go and perfume the body of Christ as an honour to their dead master and king. As they approached they were met by an angel sitting on top of the rock that was used to block the entrance to the grave where the body of Christ was supposed to be laying. The angel took them and showed them where Jesus lay before his resurrection and that he was no longer in the grave. He asked them to go and inform his disciples that they would meet him in Galilee as he had advised them before his death.

The Women's Testimony:

Straight away the women went into Jerusalem with the news of his resurrection first to his apostles and to the citizens of the city and nation. The news became the talk of the day on that beautiful Sunday. Peter and John, on hearing the news went to the grave and found that the body was indeed missing in the grave. For fear they went back into hiding but Mary remained there at the grave yard wanting to know where the Lord was and subsequently Jesus appeared to her in body calling her by her name, *"Mary" (John 20:15-16).*

The Apostles' Testimony:

"Him God raised up the third day, and shewed him

openly; Not to all the people, but unto witnesses chosen before of God, even unto us, who did eat and drink with him after he rose from the dead" (Acts 10:40-41).

Whilst his apostles went back to hiding for fear of the Jewish elders and chose to disregard the message brought by Mary that they were to meet the Lord in Galilee, the Lord himself appeared unto them. He wanted to convince them that in reality it was him risen from the dead. So he showed them his injured hands and feet and the pierced side and asked them to touch him. He ate with them to demonstrate that he had bodily form, for a spirit has no need of sustenance. The apostles needed to be convinced witnesses to his resurrection if they were to lay the first bricks on the foundations of the Church of God. Once convinced they began to spread the word of his resurrection to friends and all people they had access to. Thomas, who was absent when the Lord appeared to his fellow apostles found it difficult to believe and vowed to believe after seeing him. Jesus appeared to his disciples again in the presence of Thomas and implored him to thrust his figures right into the wounds of the Lord hands, *"And Thomas answered and said unto him, My Lord and my God." (John 20: 28).* This was a strong testimony from Thomas for the risen Christ. He knew and recognised him by those wounds inflicted for the healing and salvation of mankind. They were wounds of mercy, with which we are healed.

The Guards' Testimony:

"And for fear of him the keepers did shake, and became as dead men" (Matthew 28:4)

When the guards were placed at the sepulchre, they were to ensure that Jesus's body was not going be stolen by the disciples. They diligently did their job until the very minute when divinity took control of its plan. Suddenly there was lightning and the shaking of the earth where they stood. The stone was rolled away from the entrance to the grave by a glittering angel in white raiment. These guards were the best and most reliable witnesses who saw everything which happened at the grave that morning. God through the Jewish leaders had placed the guards to keep the grave and be the true witnesses of his resurrection to them. When the guards gained consciousness they acquired some courage and in haste left to report what they saw to their masters. As the guards narrated the truth to their masters, Satan's grip tightened on the leaders of the people. Instead of accepting and embracing the truth that indeed Jesus had risen, they instead brought out the same snare which they used for the betrayal of the Lord, "money". The difference, however was that the guards were not bought of thirty pieces of silver but *"......they gave large money unto the soldiers" (Matthew 28:12).* Satan knew what the resurrection of Jesus from the dead meant. He therefore ensured and did everything to ensure mankind doubts the resurrection of the Lord. The guards missed an opportunity to be a help to the Jews for the love of money.

The Proclamation: *Luke 24: 44-48*

Step by step and through a lot of pain and grief, Jesus accomplished the mission for which he had come to earth for, to dwell among sinful nature. With all these witnesses of his resurrection he focussed on the men who were supposed to lay the first bricks to build the Church of God. They saw him in glory as he was healing the sick, the blind, dumb and crippled. They knew him as he delivered the words of life and truth to many in Israel. They knew him at the last supper and in Gethsemane and they remembered him dragged away by the crowds and the chief priests. They knew when they abandoned him to suffer alone and Peter would remember the moment when he denied the Lord. They remembered that week-end of fear and uncertainty not only for their own lives but for the Gospel of Jesus Christ. They remembered when Mary brought the news of the Lord's resurrection and when Peter and John came back with confirmation of the missing body and when Cleopas came to say they had seen him on their way to Emmaus. When he entered the closed and locked room in body and ate with them and when he visited them to meet Thomas the doubter. All was vivid and they were beginning to appreciate and understand that in reality the Lord had risen and conquered death. Indeed all that the Lord had spoken to them about, what is written in Psalms, prophets and by Moses had been fulfilled and they were witnesses to it. In that state of mind the Lord visited to remind them of these prophesies which had been fulfilled in their eyes. The reason for all this was *"...that repentance and remission of sins should be preached in his name among all nations, beginning at Jerusalem" (Luke 24: 47)*. He said further, *"And ye are witnesses of these things"*. His apostles were the true witnesses of his sacrificial life, death and resurrection. They were the ones who were to preach repentance and remission of sins and build the church upon the laid foundation. This statement from the Lord Jesus confirms that the foundation as per God's plan had been well laid. The task was now with the apostles to build the church upon this laid foundation. If built correctly on this foundation the Gates of Hell would never prevail against it. The Gates of Hell are the sins of this world.

Said Matthew Henrys in his commentary about the Gates of Hell, *"This implies that the church has enemies that fight against it, and endeavour its ruin overthrow, here represented by the gates of hell, that is, the city of hell; (which is directly opposite to this heavenly city, this city of the living God), the devil's interest among the children of men. The gates of hell are the powers and policies of the devil's kingdom, the dragon's head and horns, by which he makes war with the Lamb; all that comes out of hell-gates, as being hatched and contrived*

33

there. These fight against the church by opposing gospel truths, corrupting gospel ordinances, persecuting good ministers and good Christians; drawing or driving, persuading by craft or forcing by cruelty, to that which is inconsistent with the purity of religion; this is the design of the gates of hell, to root out the name of Christianity (Ps. 83:4), to devour the man-child (Rev. 12:9), to raze this city to the ground.(2.) This assures us that the enemies of the church shall not gain their point. While the world stands, Christ will have a church in it, in which his truths and ordinances shall be owned and kept up, in spite of all the opposition of the powers of darkness; They shall not prevail against it, Ps. 129:1, Ps. 129:2 . This gives no security to any particular church, or church-governors that they shall never err, never apostatize or be destroyed; but that somewhere or other the Christian religion shall have a being."

A church built on the foundation laid by Jesus will overcome sin. To accept any compromise with sin is to render the cross of Jesus useless and his resurrection void. But we know in our age those born of God will not be found in any form of sin or worldliness.

CHAPTER 5

THE PENTECOST

The Instruction:

"But after I am risen again, I will go before you into Galilee" (Mathew 26:32)

Jesus instructed his disciples on what to do in each step of the journey to build the Church of God. Their success was based on obedience to each of the statutes and instruction. At the last supper before his crucifixion he instructed them to meet him in Galilee after his resurrection. Mankind often fails to obey instructions just as the disciples did at the resurrection of Jesus, where none of his disciples were either in Galilee or at the grave side. It is, however gratifying that in every situation the rich God will have someone standing out for the truth. Out of all the disciples we find Mary Magdalene not only demanding to see the risen Jesus but even wanting his dead body. Peter, a few days earlier, had vowed in front of the rest of the apostles and Jesus that though everyone else might be offended of him yet he would not be. However, as Jesus rose from the dead, Peter was hiding for his own personal safety. Jesus, though dead had become an offence as well as a source of danger to Peter. His vow had become just an empty talk. Only in a day of the death of their Lord, Peter and his fellow apostles had lost all hope and resolved to return to back to their fishing trade for a living. They went back to catch fish and trashed the divine call for them to be fishers of man *(John 21:3)*. On the other hand, it appears as if Mary and her associates had pondered since the burial of the Lord how they were going to remove the stone in order to anoint Jesus's body with precious ointment. They, however, courageously headed for the graveyard, seemingly convinced that with God's help nothing was impossible. They looked forward to divine intervention in the removal of the stone from the entrance of the sepulchre. Little did they know, nor believe, that at dawn of that Passover Sunday the Lion of Judah (Jesus) would conquer the grave. As they approached the grave the work had already been done by the workers of heaven and the big stone was off the entrance of the sepulchre with one of the workers (an angel) sitting on top of it. Desire and perseverance in faith to Jesus had conquered their burden. Nothing could deter Mary and company from seeking the face of Jesus and at last he showed himself to them. Mary and her companions became the first witnesses of the resurrection of the Lord, as per his promise to his followers and all people that he would rise on the third day.

After the Lord rose from the dead he spent some forty days meeting, teaching, reminding and convincing his disciples of the words he had taught them for three and half years. The forty days were for the sharpening and hardening of the future advocates of the Gospel of life. It is worth noting that even after this forty-day encounter with the risen Lord the disciples of Jesus remained inclined to the world. They were still Jews in thinking and yet Christ wanted them to be preachers of his word to all nations. They actually were looking forward to the restoration of the earthly kingdom of Israel saying, *"...Lord will thou at this time restore again the kingdom to Israel? (Acts 1:6).* But the Lord knew that until they received the Holy Ghost their minds would remain earthly and he had already promised to send that which would cut the connection with the world. *"And behold, I send the promise of my Father upon you: but tarry ye in the city of Jerusalem, until ye be endued with power from on high"* (Luke 24:49). Ready to depart from Earth, he knew he would not leave the disciples alone to progress the Gospel. They would forever need the presents of a member the Godhead. He had already prayed that God send the Holy

Ghost to be the teacher within the apostles and all would be preachers of the Gospel. Furthermore to this it was now high time for the disciples to know that the preaching of repentance and remission of sins is not for anyone who chooses to. They had to be qualified; not through manmade colleges but through power from on High. This was a prerequisite to their preaching of the Gospel of Jesus Christ. They could not preach repentance and remission of sins before being endued of the Holy Spirit of God. The Holy Spirit was to be their teacher, leader, reminder and comforter in the execution of the most solemn, important, delicate and often dangerous profession, which deals with the final destination of the spirit of mankind. Only supernatural power (The Holy Ghost) can convince mankind of their being sinful before God, for without this understanding repentance which lead to the salvation of the soul is impossible *(1 Corinthians 2:9-14).* This is the reason why the Lord Jesus commanded or, shall we say instructed, his disciples to stay put and not to preach until he had despatched the Holy Spirit from the father. Besides being a teacher who would teach through the medium of the disciples, the Holy Spirit was also the power for courage and fearlessness. Jesus knew that from the day he was held for crucifixion, his disciples had shown an unbelievable attitude of fear and cowardice. All were in hiding until the very day Jesus rose from the dead. Peter, the most talkative and self-confident disciple, had through fear cursed and sworn that he did not know Jesus when confronted by a damsel. For this reason Jesus told the disciples not to move from Jerusalem where he left them until he sent the promise of the father to them. This promise of the father was to be to them power to progress the Gospel without which the spreading of the Gospel would be like story telling with no tangible products. The baptism of the Holy Ghost was to qualify or licence them to start preaching the Gospel without which they would preach a counterfeit. The baptism of the Holy Ghost will remain a necessity until the end of time when the preaching of the Gospel will come to an end.

The Day of Pentecost:

"And when the day of Pentecost was fully come, they were all with one accord in one place. And suddenly there came a sound from heaven as of a rushing mighty wind, and filled all the house where they were sitting" (Acts 2:1-2)

Subsequent to the Passover feast and after fifty days came the feast of weeks or Pentecost. The Jews would gather once more to celebrate their God given harvest. They would be giving thanks to God with offerings for the new grain. Jesus ascended into heaven on the fortieth day of his resurrection and Peter with one hundred and nineteen of the disciples of Jesus gathered in a room in Jerusalem, praying and fasting in obedience to the instruction of the Lord that they were to tarry in Jerusalem until they were endured of the Holy Ghost. On the tenth day of their tarrying, which was also the first day of the feast of weeks or the Pentecost God had moulded them and made them one. We know there can never be one accord amongst a people in the absence of holiness. As they tarried in obedience to the instruction of the Lord, the Lord sanctified them in truth. Through sanctification they were bound in the spirit of oneness and God brought down the full harvest for the church. The Holy Spirit came with power and filled all of them giving each one a new language which they had never learnt to speak, speaking so fluently to the benefit of people from other nations and proselytes who had gathered to commemorate the Pentecost. Suddenly the apostles wore the full garment of salvation. Whilst they had become the children of God through salvation and sanctification, a third step took place in their spiritual lives which is the baptism of the Holy Ghost. Henceforth they were qualified to preach Jesus crucified as a saviour of mankind. In a moment fear and timidity departed from their hearts. They came out doors and openly proclaimed the news of the Gospel of Jesus Christ in the presence of the elders of Israel and in the centre of Jerusalem. They faithfully and fearlessly proclaimed the gospel even under threat of death, and indeed they died for the cause of Christ.

The Church Born.

"Be glad then, ye children of Zion, and rejoice in the LORD your God: for he hath given you the former rain moderately, and he will cause to come down for you the rain, the former rain, and the latter rain in the first month". (Joel 2:23)

This first Pentecost after the ascension of the Lord into heaven and in which the Holy Spirit fell marked the founding of the Church of God. *"And when the day of Pentecost was fully come, they were all with one accord in one place. And suddenly there came a sound from heaven as of a rushing mighty wind, and it filled all the house where they were sitting" (Acts 2:1-2)*. This was the former rain spoken of by Joel the prophet. This Spirit was never to return back to God who gave it until end of time. Over the centuries it has been poured out time and again as men and women of God surrendered their lives to God to receive him. Its continued presence has given birth to a continual revival of the church of God through difficult phases threatening its very existence. The reformation was its work and it spread like fire throughout the world. Later a large outpouring was witnessed in 1906 giving birth to a world revival, today known as the Pentecostal movement which is still gripping the world.

The full measure of the spirit which fell in Jerusalem resulted in the repentance and the salvation of three thousand souls. The Church, which is the spiritual house of God was thereby powerfully established as per the words of the Lord Jesus that repentance and remission of sins will be preached in all nations of the world starting at

Jerusalem. No Pharisee, scribe or elder of the Jews was to doubt the presence of the Church of Jesus Christ in Jerusalem. They became a force to be reckoned with. Only use of brute force and murder was to be the weapon to fight this army which had its purpose to fight the gates of hell and vanquish them. Peter said, *"This is that which was spoken by the prophet Joel" (Acts 2:16).* This windfall of the Holy Spirit had been prophesied by the prophets and the Scribes and Pharisees who were champions of the scriptures just needed to be reminded and Peter did exactly that. As per prophecy they witnessed an abundance of the Holy Spirit working in ordinary citizens of their nations. All they knew about these humble people was that they had been with Jesus. To these the Spirit fell. Whilst still wandering Peter intervened and reminded them that this was a fulfilment of what they knew. The dawn of a new era, a new dispensation was at hand. But the Jewish elders and teachers turned away from the grace so clearly given and they stuck to the covenant of the law until this day.

Peter, with his fellow apostles, preached and emphasised the grace of Jesus through faith that the Gospel is the power of God through faith to those who believe and that in it the righteousness of God is revealed. Only those penitents who were going to believe in the ability of the blood of Jesus to cleanse sin would be saved. The importance of the Law of Moses was made of no relevance to the preaching of the Gospel. The central theme was that people should repent from or leave their sinful ways so that God may forgive them. Those that heard the message and repented, that is renounce their sins in sorrow whether Jew or Gentile had their sins forgiven. Conclusively Pentecost marked a mighty change of God's dealings with mankind. Emphasis shifted from the law to grace, whilst gentiles, people out of the commonwealth of Israel were accepted as partakers of the grace in the blood of Jesus Christ. They were to be full candidates for the building of the church of God and candidates for the baptism of the Holy Ghost as long they followed the way to righteousness which is Jesus.

CHAPTER 6

WORLD EVANGELISM

The Gospel of Christ:

"Now after that John was put in prison, Jesus came into Galilee, preaching the gospel of the kingdom of God" (Mark 1:14).

Soon after John the Baptist was imprisoned by Herod Jesus immediately went into Galilee and preached the Gospel of the Kingdom of God. This was a new and universal Gospel whose aim was to gather through preaching a new citizenry of the Kingdom of God from all nations of the earth. Many of his hearers including his disciples did not understand what he was preaching about for the three and half years of his active evangelical work. This comes as the reason why as Jesus was preparing to depart from the earth after his resurrection the apostles said to him *"...Lord will thou at this time restore again the Kingdom to Israel?" (Acts 1:6).* The Israelites were already under Roman bondage. They had lost an earthly Kingdom which they expected the Messiah to restore. However, this was a misunderstanding of scripture. They believed that Christ had come to earth only for them because they still considered themselves a special people. They ignored scriptures which prophesied that Christ will come for both the Jews and the gentiles, thereby alienating themselves from the grace of God through pride and bigotry. Yes indeed the house of Israel had been chosen by God as part of his plan of salvation for the entire mankind. Through them the messiah was to be born. This messiah was to be the light of salvation to the gentile world or people who worshipped idols and to unknown gods. Jesus's birth, suffering and resurrection would bring glory to Israel as he substituted for the sins of all inhabitants of the world, him being in flesh an offspring of Israel but eternally God. Being an Israelite by birth, he was to be the mediator of a new covenant binding the whole world to its creator and at the same time abolish the old one which was for the preparation of his descent to earth. All glory would therefore be to Israel having been the custodians of the first covenant and the beginning of the new. The Kingdom of God to be established through preaching of the gospel of Jesus Christ was to be inhabited by people saved from all nations of the earth.

The Commission:

"Go ye therefore, and teach all nations, baptizing them in the name of the Father, and the Son, and of the Holy Ghost (Matthew 28:19 and 20)

Whilst the question of the apostles about the restoration of the kingdom to Israel might possibly have been a disappointment to Jesus, it, however gave him an opportunity to reinforce the fact that his mission was not for the restoration of the Kingdom of Israel but for the establishment of the Kingdom of God on Earth and that the apostles themselves will be the first builders. Now at his last hour on earth, he told them the procedure they would need to take before they embarked on the commission. They were to preach Christ under the influence and direction of the Holy Spirit for Jesus had already told them that the Holy Spirit will talk of Jesus. They were to be witnesses of Jesus in the land of Israel and eventually throughout the whole world. Under the influence of the Holy Spirit they were supposed to teach the nations to understand and observe all things he had taught and commanded them *(Acts 1:8; Matthew 28:20);* that once the people have understood the teaching they were to be baptised in the name of the Father, and of the son and of the Holy Ghost. The instruction was as crystal clear as it is in the scriptures and from the mouth of the author of our faith and covenant, Jesus Christ the saviour. No other instruction about the method of baptism was ever given before and after this instruction from the Lord. Even if someone had given another method it would be an error to deviate from the instruction of Jesus.

Therefore in Jesus's commission to his disciples, we find a clear sequence of events to be followed in the teaching of the Gospel to the nations. That is, first one has to repent which will lead them to the forgiveness of their sins through faith in Christ *(Mark 1:15)*. It is only after sins are forgiven that they ought to be baptised. All these stages have a special significance for a successful Christian life. There are diverse teachings by different church groups on these subjects but what we know is that Jesus taught only one way to salvation as stated in Mark 1: 15 and any deviation is because of the craftiness of the devil. Each subject was supposed to be taught in such a way that the penitent would understand and act accordingly in compliance to the teaching before moving to the next stage of the complete salvation.

Repentance:

"And that repentance and remission of sins should be preached in his name among all nations beginning at Jerusalem" (Luke 24: 47)

Repentance is one of the fundamentals of the Gospel of Jesus Christ, for without it forgiveness of sins remains an illusion to the penitent. Unless men or women repent of their sins they cannot be born again nor can they be saved. Repentance is the key to the free salvation of God through the blood of his son, Jesus Christ. The only price mankind can pay to purchase it is by renouncing their sins in godly sorrow. They need to turn away from their carnal and earthly behaviours voluntarily in obedience to the call of God to do so. They repent or renounce their sins because they have decided to establish an everlasting relationship with God. This repentance should not be based on any form of fear but the love of God. That message, Jesus the author of the Christian faith preached repentance in his maiden sermon. He said, *"The time is fulfilled, and the Kingdom of God is at hand: REPENT ye and believe the Gospel." (Mark 1:15).* His apostles, represented by Peter, also preached the same doctrine after the first outpouring of the Holy Spirit in Jerusalem. Repentance is part of God's plan of salvation and therefore it is a work of the grace of God. It is a product of the influence and persuasion of the Holy Spirit. It is a Godly rule and a pre-requisite to the salvation of the soul. Only God will give the repentant a desire for salvation which surpasses all profit, from that done against the will of God. This is the grace of God. Paul, on a mission to persecute Christians of Damascus met the grace of God which was waiting for him and the Spirit of God struck him down and led him to repentance. That he repented is confirmed by his words which says: *"What things were gain to me those I accounted loss for Christ,...and do count them but dung, that I may win Christ." (Philippians 3: 8-9).* Real repentance abandons the dearest for the most precious Jesus Christ. True teachers and preachers of the gospel have and will always take time to teach this fundamental as per the instruction of the Lord Jesus that it should be so. The command is to teach repentance or renunciation of own committed sin and to stop associations that lead to those sins again. God indeed overlooked at prophets and his people before who called on his name whilst they indulged in sin, but that was the old, powerless covenant of the law. God, through the advent of Christ to die for sins replaced this covenant because of its failure to make righteous. For the whole world the universal call from God is for them to repent; for without repentance there is no remission of sins. The correct way to begin the Christian journey is not by finding a new church only but repenting to God without which no one can be a Christian regardless of how much zeal they might have. Christ, who is the testator of the new covenant used wine as a symbol and said, *"For this is my blood of the new testament, which is shed for many for the remission of sins" (Matthew 26: 28)*. Indeed Jesus went ahead and shed his own blood as a fulfilment of this symbol. The expectation therefore is that from mankind sins must be remitted. It cannot be correct for anyone to call themselves followers of Christ whilst still indulging in sin of any kind. This will surely be at variance with the written word of God and the basic aim of the gospel of Christ as taught by him and his apostles. Sin and sin alone was the reason for Jesus's sacrificial death. He died to take away sin from mankind. *"And ye know that he was manifested to take away our sins; and in him is no sin." (1 John 3:5)*. That is, to make them godly, not only religious. That is why he starts by demanding that those to be his followers must repent first. Those who may claim to be Christians whilst still indulging in sin (drunkards, adulterers, fornicators, rapists, child abusers, drug addicts, liars, gossipers) are practicing what may best be described as nominal Christianity. These are people who profess to be Christians but their lives are completely at variance with what the bible teachings say. Even the bible instructs Christians to turn away from such. It will be an unforgivable betrayal of the painful death of Christ to fear to condemn wrong because the majority have decided to compromise with exactly what their purported saviour was murdered to eradicate. The only reason to join a church should be for nothing else but repentance from sin.

Repentance of the publicans:

"And Zacchaeus stood, and said unto the Lord: Behold, Lord, the half of my goods I give to the poor; and if I have taken anything from any man by false accusation, I restore him fourfold." (Luke 19: 9).

Zacchaeus was a rich man and tax collector of Jericho who

earnestly sought to see Jesus as the grace of God pushed him towards repentance. As he seemed to fail to come close enough to Jesus due to the large crowd, he put aside his stature in society as spiritual desire pushed him towards the free grace of God. As if he was confused, he climbed up a tree so as to see Jesus. He was being influenced by the boundless spirit of repentance. Like anyone who has ever been overtaken of it (the spirit of repentance), he first forgot who he was and those around him and focused on ensuring an encounter with Jesus. Jesus's divine eye can never be surpassed by such penitents. As Jesus passed by and saw Zacchaeus hanging or sitting on a tree branch, he invited him to make haste and come down so as to sup with him. Without delay Zacchaeus climbed down, not even understanding how lucky he was to get such an invitation from the Lord. The food was the word of God and the publican got the full course. Full of the Word of God, Zacchaeus began to see his wrong side of life. He began with his selfishness and went on to falsified transactions done as he performed his duty of collecting taxes for the state. His pledge was moved by the power of the grace of God to pay restitution fourfold to those robbed, in an attempt to please God and get his sins forgiven. Little did he know that the grace of God can never be purchased by money! His was not ordinary generosity but that generosity driven by the power of repentance. With this kind of repentance the Lord had no choice but to save Zacchaeus of his sins and said, *"this day is salvation come to this house......for the son of man is come to seek and to save that which was lost." (Luke 19: 1-10).* Jesus never called for Zacchaeus to be baptized in water for salvation, the only condition was repentance. Once he repented of his sins the Lord saved him. Repentance in its truest form is always accompanied by restitution, for it is impossible for a repented person to continue to sit on wrongs done to other people. The Lord Jesus taught the importance of restitution and the Old Testament is very precise about the importance of this as a requirement as well

(Exodus 22:1-17). God expects the penitents to correct all correctible wrongs which have been committed. Some may be financial, like in Zacchaeus's case and some may not be. Sinners are good at lies, gossip, malice which might have destroyed the standing and reputation of other people. If people affected are still within reach, the penitent is duty bound to correct this. All fraudulent and dishonest transactions to both individuals and companies have to be corrected as much as is possible. God will not tolerate concealment of wrongs done. *"Therefore if thou bring thy gift to the altar, and there rememberest that thy brother hath ought against thee; Leave there thy gift before the altar, and go thy way; **FIRST** be reconciled to thy brother, **and then** come and offer thy gift"* (Matt 5: 23-24).

God wants us to demonstrate a personal dislike for sin and wrong and show total faith in his ability to protect us from man's vengeance and to save us from sin.

"I will have mercy, and not sacrifice: for I am not come to call the righteous, but sinners to REPENTANCE" *(Matthew 9:13)*, said Jesus at a sermon in Matthew the publican's house. Jesus is a friend of sinners, a friendship shown through the shedding of his blood. He came to call sinners to repent as an appreciation of his sacrifice for them. He came to put a stop to the doctrine of sacrifices for he sacrificed himself for us once and it became enough. What is flowing today is his mercy to those lost in sin. If one were to lose all sins for Christ no regrets will ever follow them till eternity. A repentant person is like a brick that has gone through a furnace and is now ready to be laid on the foundation of the house of God which is Jesus Christ the Lord.

Salvation:

"For I am not ashamed of the gospel of Christ: for it is the power of God unto salvation to everyone that believeth; to the Jew first, and also to the Greek. For therein is the righteousness of God revealed from faith to faith: as it is

written, the just shall live by faith" (Romans 1:16-17).

After being almost dead for centuries, the doctrine of free Grace which was preached by Jesus Christ and his apostles was reincarnated by Martin Luther in 1517 in what we know as the Reformation. God is invisible to us. However, that God is righteous is shown through the ability of the saved to live a righteous life. This righteousness is not because those who received it have heard to labour for it, but that they have believed what they were taught and by their faith the power of God came in to reside in the hearts. God forgives the committed sins of a repentant sinner through faith in the shed blood of Jesus Christ. Renunciation of sin without believing in the ability of the Jesus to forgive sins is not useful. Faith in Jesus plays a pivotal role to communicate the state of the penitent to almighty God, who, when he finds that someone has renounced his sins, believing that God will in turn forgive him, he (God) will abundantly pardon. This blotting out of sins or regeneration will lead to a refreshed life, a new life in Christ, which is devoid of sin and worldliness. Jesus performed many miracles whilst he was still on earth but he never said the healings, casting out of demons and many other miracles would lead one to heaven. He spoke of heaven in relation to the miracle of salvation or being born again.

Nicodemus, a Pharisee and ruler of the people saw the miracles which Jesus performed coupled with his strong authoritative teachings and he was convinced that Jesus was a teacher from God. He decided to approach Jesus with words of honour, admiration and appreciation of the work he was doing and that it was not from an ordinary source. At the same time he wanted to communicate that they were many of them who believed Jesus to have come from God. Jesus, however did not waste his time with the obvious but went straight to that which Nicodemus, being a religious leader of Israel, was ignorant of. He said in answer to him, *"....except a man be born again, he cannot see the kingdom of God" (John 3:3).* So Jesus concluded that man can do anything in the name of God but unless they are born again they cannot qualify to be the citizens of his Kingdom. God gave his only begotten son that whoever believe in him should have everlasting life. For one to say they believe in Christ without the surety of entry to his kingdom is missing the purpose of why God sent Jesus to earth. The first of all things before miracles, preaching, singing or any work for God is to ensure one is born again or saved. All other works are secondary in the plan of God and cannot guarantee any relationship with the God of Heaven *(John 3:3).*

Paul and Silas were once jailed for preaching Christ. While in prison in the middle of the night, they praised God through prayer and singing until the Holy Spirit filled the jail. God, through his power caused an earthquake to shake the jail, resulting in the loosening of the door locks and doors going wide open. The prison officer thought all prisoners had escaped and, fearing the wrath of the rulers he attempted to kill himself. Paul told him that all prisoners were still in jail and there was no need for his (jailer) intended action. The jailer asked how he could be saved and Paul asked him to believe in Jesus Christ for salvation. He did not ask him to be baptised for salvation but to believe in Christ. Men and women who will repent to God by leaving their sins will be saved through faith in Christ not water baptism. I do not mean to say that water baptism has no significance in the plan of salvation, yes it has and indeed an important one as we shall see later, but baptism cannot save a man's soul but the grace of God through faith in Jesus.

It is important to note that Jesus forgives sins without the involvement of water baptism. In Mark Jesus says, *"But that you may know that the son of man hath power on earth to forgive sins...." (Mark 2: 10).* This is the Lord Jesus himself, the author of our salvation testifying that he has power to forgive sins. Again it is said, *"When Jesus saw their faith, he saith unto the sick of the palsy, Son, thy sins be forgiven thee" (Mark 2: 5).* It shows that it was this sick man who was pushing his friends and relatives to get him to Jesus for his salvation. He indeed wanted the healing of the physical body but must have been more mindful of the spiritual healing as well. This is probably the reason Jesus dealt with that which his (the cripple) faith touched first, "Salvation". The rulers and scribes hated Christ for this pronouncement and took it for pride and blasphemy. Christ never baptised any nor did he ask anyone to be baptised for the remission of their sins, however he forgave sins to many who had repented starting with Andrew, the disciple of John the Baptist. Andrew had, together with his brother and others, repented by the preaching of John Baptist and they were waiting for the Messiah to save them from their sins as they had been taught by John Baptist. Jesus finding Peter and his associates in the condition of readiness Jesus saved them and asked them to go and sin no more. He did not baptise them in order for salvation, he taught them faith in God in order to be saved. It was this that Jesus asked the apostles to go and teach all nations after which they would baptise them in the name of the Father, the Son and the Holy Ghost *(Matthew 28:19).*

Water Baptism

"Therefore we are buried with him by baptism into death: that like as Christ was raised up from the dead by the glory of the Father, even so we should also walk in the newness of life." (Romans 6:3-6).

Water baptism is not salvation neither is it for salvation, but among other things it provides the born again or saved an opportunity to openly testify to the world of his or her born again experience. It is an outward expression of an inward grace. Like circumcision, which was instituted after Abraham believed God and it was counted to him for righteousness so is baptism. Circumcision was meant to be a covenant sign of a changed life, so is baptism a covenant sign of a repentant, born again life free from sin *(Romans 6:4)*. For at salvation a penitent enters a covenant with the God. No sinful person should be baptised as their life has not changed and they have not yet entered into a covenant with God.

According to the Apostolic Faith Mission of Portland minister's manual, water baptism simply means to immerse and to baptise is to immerse a person in water and to bring him or her out again. When a person is therefore baptised in water, his or her body is immersed completely in water and brought out again. As a foundational symbol of Christianity water baptism means or represents the death, burial and resurrection of Jesus. Jesus himself was baptised to fulfil all righteousness by foretelling his coming death, burial and resurrection *(Matthew 3:5)*. That in like manner a Christian through repentance and salvation has died and resurrected with Christ. Therefore people who have become Christians through salvation are baptized in order to identify with Jesus in body, spirit and soul before the world. It is such a vow in which they are saying openly to the world that even the gates of hell cannot prevail against them because they are born again. The saved will by baptism reckon themselves to be dead to sin and sin cannot reign in their mortal bodies. The bodies which die and which were before salvation are subject unto all sins. Many would justifiably ask why God sent John the Baptist to baptise in water. Yes, John did baptize, but his baptism was for repentance in preparation for the salvation which was to be preached by Jesus Christ. Only Jesus was manifested to take away sin as the scriptures clearly say. John's ministry was to prepare people for the remission of sins at the arrival of Jesus. He taught them the highest level of repentance which is accompanied by restitution and being charitable, *"Then said he to the multitude that came forth to be baptized of him, O generation of vipers, who hath warned you to flee from the wrath to come? Bring forth therefore fruits worthy of repentance, and begin not to say within yourselves, We have Abraham to our father: for I say unto you, That God is able of these stones to raise up children unto Abraham. And now also the axe is laid unto the root of the trees: every tree therefore which bringeth not forth good fruit is hewn down, and cast into the fire. And the people asked him, saying, What shall we do then? He answereth and saith unto them, He that hath two coats, let him impart to him that hath none; and he that hath meat, let him do likewise. Then came also publicans to be baptized, and said unto him, Master, what shall we do? And he said unto them, Exact no more than that which is appointed you. And the soldiers likewise demanded of him, saying, And what shall we do? And he said unto them, Do violence to no man, neither accuse any falsely; and be content with your wages" (Luke 3: 7-14).* The foregoing verse precisely sums up John Baptist mission. At the climax of his ministry John baptised Jesus for a threefold purpose. Firstly it was to fulfil ALL righteousness NOT to bring it about, (Matthew 3: 15) as Jesus was already righteous. Secondly, it was done to introduce Jesus to the world. (John 1:29-34) Thirdly, Jesus was baptised as a prophecy for his death, burial and resurrection as already has been mentioned.

Paul on Baptism:

"For Christ sent me not to baptize, but to preach the gospel: not with wisdom of words, lest the cross of Christ should be made of none effect" (1 Corinthians 1:17).

Paul was one of the greatest preachers of the first century and made countless disciples during his ministry. He openly declared that Christ never sent him to baptise but to preach the Gospel. If indeed baptism was a fundamental for salvation Paul would have baptised every convert that came his way but he just baptised a few and seriously downplayed the ceremony of water baptism. How could Paul, a minister of such stature before God do this? The reason is simple; water baptism is not a necessity for salvation. It is not! Baptism into the body of Christ is the necessity and it is called salvation. Paul's emphasis as with the rest of the apostles was on preaching the Gospel of Jesus Christ for the Gospel is the power to save through the enlightening of the Spirit and the word. The death, burial and resurrection of Jesus Christ for our sins define what the Gospel is and that water baptism has no place in this definition.

The Thief on the Cross:

"..Today shalt thou be with me in paradise" (Luke 23: 39-43).

When Jesus died on the cross he had two murderers on each side also hanging on their crosses. One of them confessed that Jesus was Lord and asked for his sins to be pardoned right at the point of death. Jesus forgave the sins of the murderer and assured him that he will be in paradise which is the Kingdom of God with him. If water baptism was a necessity for salvation, how could Jesus promise paradise to the dying murderer? He could have told him that it was too late as there was no time for him to be baptised. But because water baptism has no part in the salvation of the soul the repentant sinner was baptised into the body of Christ by the Holy Spirit and became fit for paradise immediately on the cross, so is the power and simplicity of salvation through the blood of Jesus Christ. We do not need the Jordan River to be saved, but instead the riven side of Jesus.

Sanctification:

"I have given them thy word; and the world hath hated them, because they are not of the world, even as I am not of the world. I pray not that thou should take them out of the world, but that thou should keep them from the evil.

54

They are not of the world, even as I am not of the world.
Sanctify them through thy truth: thy word is truth."
(John 17: 14-17).

Towards the end of his earthly ministry Jesus prayed to God that his disciples might be sanctified. This was a significant prayer indeed which introduced a new phase in the progression of the disciples' Christianity. Here, Jesus reveals the prevailing state of his disciples spiritually and physically. That through salvation brought about by the washing of water in the word, they like him were no more of the world, regardless of them still being residents of the earth physically. He reiterates and confirms the truth that he who is born of God or saved is separated from sin and worldliness. He, however, did not want them taken out of the world as they were to be his ambassadors on earth. He through prayer entreated God to perform another work on them so as to ensure they were able to resist worldliness and be kept from its influence. He asked God for their sanctification in the truth of the word. Sanctification would remove the earthly characteristic from within their hearts and make them pure in heart, unworldly and anti-world like their master Jesus Christ. Sanctification is a work of the grace of God through the blood of Jesus Christ *"Wherefore Jesus also, that he might* **sanctify** *the people with his own BLOOD, suffered without the gate." (Hebrews 13:12).* So Jesus went to suffer at Calvary's cross not only to save but in order to sanctify people; in other words, not only to forgive but to make holy. Just as salvation has as its task the creation of a new creature, sanctification was to cleanse the heart of mankind from all dirt ever attributed to it. This was the absolute love of God shown through the rough and painful cross of Calvary. Through the cross Jesus gave himself without measure that he might save and sanctify the church.

This doctrine which was laid down by Jesus was also preached by his disciples. Paul, emphasizing the importance of the work of sanctification, said Christ loved the church to the extent of dying for it, *"That he might* **Sanctify** *and* **Cleanse** *it with the washing of water by the word, That he might present it to himself a glorious church, not having spot or wrinkle, or any such thing; but that it should be holy and without blemish." (Ephesians 5:25-27).* This therefore shows that the cleansing power of the plan of salvation is in sanctification. God wants a perfect church in heaven, never to be cheated of the devil again. For this reason therefore it becomes imperative that every Christian should seek to be sanctified. During the period under the reformation John Wesley the Methodist preacher believed the doctrine of *entire sanctification* and in his book *Christian Perfection* referred to sanctification as his church's distinctive gift to Christianity. He called it "the great promise of God". Put correctly it was Christ's gift to Christianity which had just gone out of existence. It was therefore God's gift to the church. However by the grace of God John Wesley should be credited for resurrecting this doctrine after it had been buried for centuries, in the process depriving the church of one of its foundational doctrines. Because of the spiritual devotion and consecrations required to attain to the grace of sanctification, the Christian world has been guilty of neglecting this doctrine. This should never be the case, for heaven is for the holy and only the sanctified are holy. In our present Pentecostal age the same doctrine was again resurrected at the Azusa street 1906 revival. Since then it has been preached and many have lived and are still living a holy life. If for the some reason this doctrine goes silent again God will ensure that he will through his Holy Spirit bring it back to life until the end of time.

Sanctification entails self-search and correction of wrongs done before. Ill-gotten wealth and advantage has to be forsaken in order for God to grant this high order of Christianity. Self is killed and humbleness exercised.

Sanctification is not a progression brought about by experience and works but a work of grace and faith like salvation, born out of one's deep desire for the deeper

56

things of God. Many scriptures testify of men and women who were holy and pleased God. *"By faith Enoch was translated that he should not see death; and was not found, because God had translated him: for before his translation he had this testimony, that he pleased God." (Hebrews 11:5)*. It is important for the whole world to know that the salvation that is brought about by the death of Christ is complete and thorough and has the ability to produce men and women who can never compromise with sin under any circumstance. The fact that so many Christians refused to recant their faith under the most barbaric persecution testifies of the influence the power God has on the sanctified. They sealed the truth of the salvation through faith in the blood of Christ by their own blood.

Baptism of the Holy Ghost:

"I indeed baptize with water unto repentance: but he that cometh after me is mightier than I, whose shoes I am not worthy to bear: he shall baptise you with the Holy Ghost, and with fire" (Matthew 3:11).

This was John the Baptist as he was preaching in the wilderness of Judea. Water baptism was used by John the forerunner to Jesus Christ as a sign of repentance for the remission of sins. Jesus Christ did not continue this practice and neither did his disciples. However as already seen water baptism remains relevant to the solid foundation of Godliness only as an outward expression of an inward performed work. It is therefore meant for the saved not for the repenting. Jesus Christ was however going to baptise all those who have become sanctified Christians with the Holy Ghost for two reasons.

Firstly, the Word says, *"I will pray the father and he shall give you another Comforter, that he may abide with you forever; even the Spirit of truth which the world cannot receive, because it seeth him not, neither knoweth him: but ye know him; for he dwelleth with you, and shall be in you. But the Comforter which is the Holy Ghost, whom the father will send in my name, he shall teach you all things, and bring all things to your remembrance, whatsoever I have said unto you." (John 14:16, 17, 26).* In the life of a saved and sanctified Christian, the preceding scriptures state clearly and precisely why they need to be baptised of the Holy Ghost. He (Jesus) was about to depart and leave them in a world of temptations, tribulations and pain. Whilst he was with them he could comfort and encourage them through all these difficulties. But he was about to depart to heaven. The Holy Ghost which was going to dwell in their cleansed hearts was to give them comfort in pain, persecution and even execution by the enemy of the cross. He (the Holy Ghost) will remind them of the words of the Lord Jesus Christ whilst he was yet with them both for their comfort and to pass on to those they were to preach to. Through them the Holy Ghost with his power of conviction would speak to the wider world about the resurrected saviour Jesus Christ, who was able to redeem them from sin and disease through grace in his blood and at last to receive them in the New Heaven and New earth. Only the Holy Ghost would be qualified for such teaching as he was from God like Christ.

Secondly the Word says, *"Behold I send the promise of my father upon you: but tarry ye in Jerusalem, until ye be endued with power from on high," (Acts 24:49).* Meaning that though sanctified man without the indwelling of the Holy Spirit remains powerless in the execution of the things of God, more so the preaching of the Gospel. Besides there is always needless fear in a soul not baptised in the Holy Ghost yet the bible states that the fearful will not inherit the Kingdom of God. Fear is a danger to the Christian as demonstrated by Peter during Jesus trial. Fear led him to the sin of lying, cursing and hiding away from the truth. Flesh and blood as they cannot inherit the Kingdom of God, they also cannot alone represent God on earth. Therefore if man has to represent God, they will need the indwelling of his Spirit. This is the *"Spirit of truth" (John 16:13)* in which they have to be baptised.

Peter and his associates demonstrated the truth of this statement a mere fifty days after they ran away from people who were not after arresting them. They could boldly face those who wanted to behead them soon after being baptised of the Holy Ghost and fire from on high.

Conclusively baptism of the Holy Ghost is not optional to a Christian, for there will be no success in the things of God without his indwelling comfort, guidance, teaching and power. The mistake of not consecrating enough for baptism of the Holy Ghost to be realised, witnessed by speaking in tongues has resulted in the Christians losing the precious gifts of the cross which are salvation and sanctification. Baptism of the Holy Ghost is therefore an indispensable pillar of the foundation of Godliness without which the house of God cannot stand. As with the other foundational doctrines, baptism of the Holy Ghost was preached by Jesus apostles. John Wesley speaking about the Holy Spirit said that "without the Spirit, the Word is a dead letter, and without the Word the Spirit flutters as an illusion". He, as one of the preachers at the time of the Reformation was emphasizing on the indispensability of the Holy Spirit to a Christian. It was the outpouring of the Holy Spirit under the teaching of William Seymour in 1906 which ignited the Pentecostal revival that is still raging like wild fire in different parts of the world in our age. There has never been a revival without first the outpouring of the Holy Spirit, and there shall never be.

Devine Healing:

"I drew them with cords of a man, with bands of love." *(Hosea 11:4).*

Another part of the brick and mortar of the foundation of the Gospel of Jesus Christ is love and mercy. Christ from the onset designed to draw people to himself not by the use of force or coercion but instead by the bands of love and grace unfeigned. He was to draw them to himself with the cords and bands of love. This was the attraction which was to make them run to him. Therefore as Jesus began to preach and teach the Gospel to mankind he also began to work on their physical wellbeing. His mission and commission had imbedded into it the cure and healing of physical and spiritual maladies. Sin is a disease, a sickness and a torment and Christ came to take away sin. Jesus was aware that people's immediate need was the healing of their bodies. The whole plan of salvation was therefore designed to meet the penitent on their own ground. He healed all manner of disease, sickness and cast out devils or evil spirits. The news of a divine teacher and healer spread like wildfire in all lands of the Jews and beyond. This fame brought people of all ages, nations and tongues to Jesus. It is said, *"Jesus went about all Galilee, teaching in their synagogues and preaching the Gospel of the kingdom, and healing all manner of sickness and all manner of disease among the people", (Matthew 4: 23-24)*. As they gathered to be healed the Spirit of God also made them understand that many of the diseases were a direct result of the sins of the sick. Jesus taught them that a renunciation of sin will result in the healing of the body as well. Hearing this, many responded and found the teaching to be true. As they gave up their evil ways their bodily maladies also disappeared. Many brought their sick relatives seeking for healing and as they listened to the teaching they found themselves to be sick because of sin. They would then seek for salvation as well. As part of his commission to the disciples after his resurrection from the dead and just before his ascension to heaven Jesus reaffirmed that healing of the sick should always be part of the preaching of his Gospel on Earth, *"they shall lay hands on the sick and they shall recover" (Mark 16: 15-18)*. The preaching of the Gospel of Christ should always be accompanied by the healing of sickness as the immediate proof or product of the presents of supernatural power working through the preacher. This healing through faith in Jesus does not segregate between diseases as with

60

human healers but will heal "all manner of sickness and disease" which will ever attack mankind on earth.

In conclusion it can be seen that the foundation of God upon which he is building his church includes both the spirit of mankind and their fleshly bodies. The whole person must take part in order for him or her to be godly. Only those built on the foundational doctrines above will succeed in their endeavour to please God Almighty. Pleasing God is not natural but rather supernatural. As seen above, these teachings are universal as taught by the Lord, his apostles and later by various messengers of God at different times in the history of the Church. It is therefore not the aim of the writer to introduce a new manifesto but to emphasise to people of this generation the importance of these foundational principles upon which Christianity is built, lest they are trashed for unscriptural and simplistic teachings. Only after having earnestly understood these doctrines and subsequently being born again, did the writer start to enjoy the sweetness of the Gospel of Christ. It has been a pleasant 32 years of living in Christ.

CHAPTER 7

THE LIFE BUILT ON THE FOUNDATION

We have seen in the foregoing chapters how God fulfilled his plan to build the foundation of godliness after the fall in Eden. All the events from the call of Abram to the resurrection and ascension of Christ were the material with which God built the foundation of godliness. How should they, who are built on such a foundation, be found conducting their life on Earth? It is expected that this life will be completely at variance with lives built on other foundations.

The Spiritual Life:

"Ye are the salt of the earth....." (Matthew 5:13)

Christianity is a practical reality and not an illusion. It is indeed a way of life. All the foundational doctrines explained in the foregoing chapters are a creation of God to enable a Christian to practically live a righteous and holy life on Earth, for that is the purpose for which Christ came. Whilst these doctrines have suffered a lot of attacks and misinterpretations over the centuries, they have always resurfaced with greater power and results. As we have already seen reformers like Martin Luther, John Wesley, and lately William Seymour with many of their contemporaries brought the sometimes dormant Christian doctrines to life at different periods of time. Just as Jesus and the apostles emphasised on the importance of the foundational doctrines as a means to the salvation of Christ and resultant exemplary lives of believers, these later day men and women of God emphasised the same. Jesus likened the saved person to the salt of the earth, which means that if someone is saved they are given the ability to make the tasteless lives of others become meaningful. They spread hope instead of despair and discouragement. They are the conduit through which the depressed and broken hearted are restored. Jesus also likened the saved to the light of the earth as opposed to the dark world of sin in which we live. Their lives will show the beauty of accepting Christ as one's personal saviour, by their long-suffering, patient and blameless conduct in the society in which they leave. Paul the apostles said the Christian's life is like an epistle which mankind can read and understand how God is able to remould the lives of individuals. The character of God cannot be clearly understood through the theoretical but true writings in the bible, hence the life of a Christian is meant to be a practical demonstration of the infallibility, righteousness and accuracy of the Word of God.

To be a Christian is a mystery. The Word says, *"for ye are the temple of the living God; as God hath said, I will dwell in them, and walk in them; and I will be their God, and they shall be my people"* (2 Corinthians 6:16). A temple is the place where God dwells. It is a place set aside for God. No one is expected to dwell in a temple as it is reserved for God. In the dispensation of Grace in which we are God has no dwelling place in manmade temples? Manmade temples were a symbol of that which was to come as the prophecy says. That which was to come was the issuing of a brand new heavenly heart and spirit replacing the old corruptible, earthly and worldly heart and spirit at regeneration, *"A new heart will I give you, and a new spirit will I put within you...."* (Isaiah 36:26a). This change of heart and spirit enables God to find a place to dwell in the heart of mankind. God, the Holy Spirit flows in immediately once a holy temple is created in a man or woman by the works of justification and sanctification. He goes in to set up his headquarters in the new godly heart. The Christian man or woman therefore becomes a captive to the will of God as God from the headquarters, which is the heart, dictates what one has to do or not do. A kingdom of God free of corruption, sin and malice is created in the heart of the Christian. Consequently that new practical life will then agree with the scriptures which says: *"Whosoever abideth in him sinneth not…." (John 3: 6).* Therefore in a Christian is achieved the aim for which God sent his son. The type of Christianity where mankind still indulge in sin has no part in the plan of God. It is that house which the word of God says is built on a sandy foundation, for any small wind will pull it down. The wind referred to is sin.

Amazing Grace:

*"Of which Salvation the prophets have inquired and searched diligently who prophesied of the **Grace** that should come unto you" (1 Peter 1: 10).*

The prophets of old were zealous of good works. They knew the scriptures and were given scriptures not through reading like we do today but direct from the Holy Spirit. They therefore through the Holy Ghost came to know what God's plans for mankind were. They knew God was planning to restore a permanent purity of the Garden of Eden in the human heart. They knew of the messiah who was to come for this restoration of the kingdom of God. The prophets were convinced about this plan and desired to be partakers of it too. In this desire driven from understanding the meaning, power and result of this Salvation they started to inquire and to search with diligence on when it was to be ushered on earth. Like treasure seekers of this world, they inquired of the source of this salvation and how to get to it. They understood that our salvation would be the direct consequence of the Grace of God, for he was going to pay the price for our sins. But God told them that this salvation was reserved for you and me of this later generation. The Prophets had this heavy heart because whilst they worshiped God and understood the statutes and commandments of God, they failed to attain to the standard which they knew salvation would take mankind to. They remained in a state of sinfulness and worldliness and yet they also understood through the Holy Ghost that there was a Salvation from God able to rescue mankind from these calamities. But God by his own wisdom denied them the salvation and reserved it for you and me.

They understood that out of this salvation born out of the suffering of Christ will flow rivers of Glory and wells of living water. That free salvation will be offered to sinners yet prophets could not access it. The prostitute of Samaria was found of this grace. Whilst she was in the act of sin, in the very act Grace dawned and overwhelmed her. Grace, Amazing Grace made her to confess her sins to Jesus Christ. When asked to go and bring her husband she said, *"I have no husband.."* (John 4: 17). Who made her to confess? No one but the Grace of God did it. For when grace takes hold of sinners, its work is to make them abandon the sins through confession and at times restitution. For without this decisive action the Grace of God cannot take hold on its prey. Saul of Tarsus was breathing out threats and slaughter against the disciples of the Lord, but as he neared Damascus, the Amazing grace of God with its mighty power to kill the flesh and resurrect the spirit, struck him down. Whilst like dead he heard the Grace say to him that it was hard for him to kick against the pricks. Grace is not resistible neither is it by choice but by its own power that man and women find it, so that no one can boast of having found it by their own means. It is a priceless gift for the price was paid by the precious blood of Jesus Christ at Calvary's cross. Waking up from that heavy blast of Grace, Saul's life was changed which he signified by a change of name to Paul. Instead of a king, he became a servant of the people. A murderer became a healer, a liar became a honeycomb of truth, a Pharisee; a symbol of deceit became an apostle an agent of Grace. Later on, like any who fall into this Grace, Paul says, *"And herein do I exercise myself, to have always a conscience*

65

void of offence toward God and toward men" (Acts 24:16). This kind of conscience can only be a direct result of Salvation. That is why the Prophets inquired and searched diligently of this Salvation. They came to understand that the results of this salvation would be so glaringly and wondrously unique that even the creatures of Heaven would also want to look into them. John Newton many centuries after Paul, Peter and all the apostles and many centuries before us also understood practically the works of this Salvation and said in his song (1779),

"Amazing Grace"
The earth shall soon dissolve like snow,
The sun forbears to shine,
But God who called me hear below,
Will be forever mine.

In the Similitude of a Vine:

"I am the vine, ye are the branches: He that abideth in me, and I in him, the same bringeth forth much fruit: for without me ye can do nothing" (John 15:1-8)

Christ's method of teaching his Gospel was meant to simplify it that anyone who had the desire to understand it could do so easily. For he says, *"For my yoke is easy and my burden is light" (Matthew 11:28).* The Gospel is meant to redeem and to take the burden off our spiritual and earthly shoulders. It is meant to brighten our understanding and not to confuse. In Chapter 15 of John we see Jesus with his disciples, teaching them about the direct product of his Gospel so that they could ensure they have the power of it and not get confused or confuse others after his departure to Heaven.

In his teaching he used the similitude or analogue of a vine tree. Christ represents himself as the true vine. As the true vine he has the roots which bears the trunk and through which the whole tree depends for its survival. The

66

Christian is here represented as a branch. As in a tree, the branch grows out of the tree trunk and it depends on the tree for its food and drink. The unity between the tree and the branch is such that it is impossible for the tree to eat or drink without the branch eating and drinking as well. It therefore follows that the fruit which the branch produces depends entirely on the food it gets from the tree for its quality and quantity. Jesus, in emphasis said he was the vine and the Christians are the branches to that vine tree. Their condition for reproduction was in them ensuring they abide in Jesus the vine and he in turn would abide in them. The result of that relationship would be many fruits, the fruits of righteousness. However, he declares that without him one cannot do anything related to Christianity even if they profess to be so. This is a defining statement in terms of the reproduction of the fruits of Christianity. We need to remember that in this entire discourse God Jehovah is the husbandman, in other words the owner, of the field. He is the one watching with an eagle's eye and tending the vine to ensure that it produces the desired quality of grape fruits.

The Godhead has complete faith and trust in Jesus Christ as the true vine upon which all branches will grow. From the earthly vine in the fields of this world of ours we seek for grapes and nothing more, as from a Christian we seek for the fruits of Christianity and nothing more. The abundance of fruit from a Christian referred to by the Lord as "much fruit" are righteousness, holiness, love, peace, joy, truthfulness, gentleness, longsuffering, meekness, humbleness and everything associated with goodness. To a Christian lies, gossip, backbiting, adultery, fornication, homosexuality, hypocrisy, deceit or any such works associated with the devil are wild fruits with which they should never be associated. A Christian's life, conversation and disposition must declare him or her to be a child of God. A disciple of Jesus Christ must be fruitful through the power in the Cross of Jesus Christ. There is no two ways about it. It is when Christians are in this state that it becomes possible for them to diffuse and spread the true message of salvation. Just like the vine which diffuses and spreads food and water to the branches for them to bear fruit, a Christian diffuses and spreads righteousness to the world. If there is no water and nutrients going up the trunk and branches of a vine it withers and die. In the same manner if the Christian fails to feed on the word of the cross, which is the true water of the soul of mankind, their Christianity withers and die. Christians ought to feed on the word of God through, prayer, reading and studying the word and listening to sermons, all under the sure influence of the Holy Spirit.

The branch must abide and be secured on the vine without which it cannot survive. The branch depends entirely on the vine for its survival just as the Christian depends entirely on Christ for his or her survival. Without Christ there is no fruit for a Christian. It is the cross of Christ which fertilizes for the production of the fruit of righteousness. This is the truth upon which success in the Christian journey can only be achieved! A Christian's exemplary living will bring many to Christ but a careless life will drive many away. This is an undisputable truth. Faithfulness to God is a great blessing beyond comparison, for it brings Glory to God and pulls many to the true discipleship of Christ. This fruitfulness and reproduction is the true evidence of being in Christ for we can do nothing without him.

No Compromise:

Christians must put on a unique standard set apart from other religions in order to differentiate themselves from anything that is called religion or worshipped on earth. This differentiation should be through the attractive, life-changing characteristics of this wonderful religion called Christianity. It is not a secret that there are nations and people who hate Christianity to the core, not of their fault but because of the behaviour of Christians now and over the centuries. Christianity has been abused and misrepresented and until today it is still under this attack not by people of other religions but by the very professors of the Christian religion. These are the real enemies of it and hence the real enemies of God. Christians of all persuasions, be it Catholic, Protestants or the modern day Pentecostal have failed and are still failing Christianity. This failure may be attributed to carelessness and ignorance of the scriptures by the professors of Christianity but the biggest enemy is compromise with sin and the world. The quest to be accepted by the world coupled with love for money and riches is at the core of the systematic destruction of Christianity and its values. The real Gospel of Christ based on the truth of the bible is being sacrificed in order for the proponents of religion to be fitting nuts in the world of sin. Ministers, bishops and the like accept and become advocates of the evils of the world instead of being enemies to it. It is a fact that the true church of God will not agree with the governments of this world on fundamental Christian standards. This disagreement was the major reason for many persecutions endured by Christians, since the first century A.D. Christians were murdered, imprisoned and tortured whilst they stood firm for what they believed in and knew to be true. They died in faith and for their faith. At times they went into hiding, lived in catacombs or migrated to far lands seeking the freedom to worship God in spirit and truth. They shed their own blood, losing all that belonged to them including dignity as they refused to accept the wrong dictates of a church compromised by its unity to the earthly governments. At last the separation of the church and government resulting in guarantees on freedom of worship was achieved through bloody sacrifices. Over the years this freedom has been eroded and gradually compromised. Governments, especially those in the West, are going back again to enforce some laws which are clearly at strong variance with the teachings of the bible and the church. A good example is the gay laws where homosexuals are by force of law able to adopt children against the wishes of the church and the Christian faith. A situation has been created over the last few years where society is being forced by law to accept same-sex partnerships and marriages against their own beliefs and the bible. Due to the power and influence of the members of the gay and lesbian society other people's rights are being overlooked and discarded to give way to practices which they believe to be evil and unacceptable to their faith and practices. It cannot be considered extreme for a true Christian to be strongly against the practice of homosexuality since the bible is explicit on what it categorises it (homosexuality) to be. *"Thou shalt not lie with mankind, as with women kind: it is an abomination" (Leviticus 18:22).* It is an abomination or a violation of the Christian or Godly norms. This is what the Christian's book of law categorically states and what any true Christian should stand for. Some may argue and say this was a statute from the old covenant but that would not be correct as the following new covenant scripture states. *"Wherefore God also gave them up to uncleanness through the lusts of their own hearts, to dishonor their own bodies between themselves: Who changed the truth of God into a lie…… For this cause God gave them up unto vile affections: for even their women did change their natural use into that which is against nature: And likewise also the men, leaving the natural use of the woman, burned in their lust one toward another; men with men working that which is unseemly, and receiving in themselves that recompense of their error which was meet. And even as they did not like to retain God in their knowledge, God gave them over to a reprobate mind, to do those things which are not convenient" (Romans 1:24-28).* The foregoing sums up why the GLB movement has gained so much popularity and support and why it threatens to rupture the churches. It is a result of the world changing the truth of God into a lie and refusal of mankind to retain God in their minds. The devil therefore took control of them and led them into these abominations. To a Christian, however the practice of ho-

70

mosexuality remains as immoral as murder, prostitution, theft where the bibles categorises it. As Christians we do not hate homosexuals just as we would not hate others who practice the other vices but we refuse to accept the practitioners as Christians. We pray that God may lead them to see the light and repent just as we pray for prostitutes and thieves, for they are in the same category before God. They are all the reason why Jesus came to earth. There has never been a time when church members demanded for practising prostitutes to be bishops. It is therefore a wonder why some people would choose to single out only one vice for such recognition in the church of God.

The argument that homosexuality is due to genetics can equally be said of prostitution if an attempt is made to investigate, but to a Christian this will still remain an abomination because the bible says so.

If the church on Earth was true it should normally be united on this issue. However as we know this is not the case. It is on record that Bishop Desmond Tutu of South Africa said he would refuse to go to heaven where homosexuals are not permitted!(BBC News Africa, 26th July, 2013) This is clear blasphemy by a man who should know better and be guiding the world to God if he was sticking to his ordination. However it is also a fulfilment of scripture which says, *"Having a form of godliness, but denying the power thereof: from such turn away" (2 Timothy 3:5).* Christians cannot be moved by such utterances but must actually stand more resilient to the truth.

Own Righteousness:

"And be found in him, not having mine own righteousness, which is of the law, but that which is through the faith of Christ, the righteousness which is of God by faith" (Philippians 3:9)

When one is saved he is led of the Spirit of God. They are

imbedded in the Gospel of Christ in which the righteousness of God is revealed through their way of living. Therefore the righteousness which they possess is in fact not theirs. It is imputed or borrowed righteousness. It is not derived from the ability to keep the law of God but from faith in Jesus Christ. God is righteous and those who worship him in spirit and truth will also be made righteous through faith in the shed blood of Christ. The law was never meant to redeem but to condemn so that mankind can discover themselves that they are law breakers, hence sinful and have need to repent. The law was the road to repentance. To claim to be righteous because of an ability to keep the law is indeed an own righteousness which has never been achieved since Sinai. God's people, men and women desired to be holy and righteous but in vain. The salvation through the faith of Christ is the only source of righteousness ever given to mankind. The righteousness so planted will equip one with the power not to break God's or man's laws. When one breaks man's laws deliberately it is a testimony of an unregenerate heart. Unless man's law is pushing one to sin a righteous person will never attempt to break it. They are a very patient, long-suffering lot who are planted by God to demonstrate his patience on earth. God is patient and long-suffering else he would have destroyed the world long back. The righteous have the same spirit which is in God because they are themselves living in God. They are given power to be God's children and become brothers and sisters to Jesus. They become rivers of living water imparting righteousness to the spiritually needy and are also a ready source of help to the materially less privileged. Jesus was the Lord of giving to the hungry and poor. He never came short on that duty. The righteous will always follow along the Jesus way, not because of material abundance but their spiritual status persuades them to act like their Lord Jesus. They are a honeycomb of good works. They do not give to please God but to be like God who freely gave his son to us the spiritually needy. Christ is the hope and source of mankind's spiritual and moral living and Christians are his true ambassadors on earth.

Knowing him:

"That I may know him" (Philippians 3: 10a.)

To know Christ is to put on Christ, to wear him in spirit and body. He becomes our everyday protection from the treachery and attractions of this world. *"For as many of you as have been baptised into Christ have put on Christ" (Galatians 3:27).* To know Christ is to walk in newness of life showing we have died from our sins with him. That as his body was crucified on the cross at Calvary, we through faith have also heard our bodies crucified, buried at baptism and raised in newness of a sinless life. Without this radical change of life one cannot be counted as having any part with Christ regardless of position in church or profession. A Christian needs to know Christ through a change of life not through their word of mouth. A child in a family must be easily identified by the features which resemble the parents. Passers-by will testify without being told that indeed this boy or girl belongs to this family because they have features resembling their father and mother. *"And because you are sons, God has sent forth the Spirit of his Son into your hearts, crying, Abba, Father." (Galatians 4: 6).* Christians must also be characteristically identical to God. Once we are sons, God sends the same Spirit that is in his son and our Lord Jesus Christ into our centre of control, the heart, so that the Spirit which controls and leads Christ becomes the Spirit which controls those that are adopted into the family of God through salvation which is by Faith. They can like Jesus cry to God as their Father and he will say "Here I am" God can hear them and they can hear God. They know God as their father and like Christ will die to do his will. Christ said, when faced with the most fearful moment of his earthly life, he said *"Oh my Father, if this cup may not pass away from me, except I drink it, thy will be done"* (Matthew 26: 42). To know Christ is to reach this level of closeness to God, where God's will comes first before our will. That once we know what we are doing is God's will, to pursue it to its conclusive end even if it means death to the flesh, knowing that the flesh may indeed die but our souls will be preserved in safety by doing God's will. Shadreck, Misheck and Abednigo and their fellow captive Daniel knew God. Through this knowledge and faith they did not run away from the furnaces of fire and the dens of lions, but rather entreated God to quench the violence of fire and stop the mouths of lions for them. When the apostles came to know Jesus they questioned their enemies who were demanding that they should not speak nor teach in the name of Jesus. They steadfastly went on preaching Christ and indeed many were murdered for their faith.

The Power of his Resurrection:

"For if we have been planted together in the likeness of his death, we shall also in the likeness of his resurrection" (Romans 6:5).

Jesus died to destroy sin, was buried to bury the power of sin and raised to conquer sin. The power of sin is in its ability to kill, as the word says, *"The sting of death is sin ..." (1 Corinthians 15:56).* If Jesus had failed to resurrect from the dead the plan of salvation would have failed. But praise be to God that Jesus rose from the dead on the third day of his death. The power of sin is to ensure people die forever. But by rising from the dead Jesus defied the law of sin which is death. The grave was made powerless. The first victim of the resurrection of Jesus was death, meaning those with the Spirit of God would no longer die. Only the saved would have the Spirit of Jesus Christ and therefore become the sons of God. These like Jesus are excluded from the second death and they will have part in the first resurrection at the tramp of God. *"Blessed and holy is he that hath part in the first resurrection: on such the second death hath no power......" (Revelation 20: 6).* This is the power in Jesus's resurrection, the total annihilation of death and its power.

Those who are risen with Christ come out of the grave wearing a body that is anti-sin, anti-world and with an affection that is towards heaven. They have such a life that is hidden in God like Christ. They seek to be one day at the right hand of God with the Lord Jesus. They believe and know that they are no longer of the world as Christ declares them to be *"They are not of the world, even as I am not of the world." (John 17: 16).* They have become through faith a people of hope beyond the grave striving day and night to conform to the word of God through the urging of the Holy Ghost which dwells in their hearts. They are prisoners of their own faith in God, being certain that when he (Jesus) shall appear the second time, they shall be like him and shall see him as he is. The power of Jesus's resurrection will make the proponents of it believe and confirm through their actions and lives that they are strangers and pilgrims on earth and seek a better country wherein dwell righteousness. These people are they who will have no time to look back to the world of sin, instead they mortify the bodies. They practice discipline and subjugation of their bodily desires, through the power they were given by the salvation of Jesus Christ so as to deny the body of its physical appetites. The power of the resurrection of Christ is the mortifying power which is able to engage the body into submission against all its physical appetites of deception, fornication, covetousness, adultery, concupiscence, idolatry and others. The mouth or tongue is through the power of the resurrection of Christ bridled to speak no guile and malice. For out of a wicked heart cometh anger, wrath, malice, blasphemy, lies and all bad communication. These are works from an old unrepentant life. No one should claim to know Jesus if they are still a slave to these fleshly traits, for in Jesus's death and resurrection is found the power to subdue them all. These activities or rather vices are a preserve of the children of disobedience not members of the church of God.

Fellowship of his Suffering:

"Wherefore Jesus also, that he might sanctify the people with his blood, suffered without the gate." (Hebrews 13:12).

We fellowship with Christ in glory, in healing, in salvation, in the baptism of the Holy Ghost. What a fellowship, it is so wonderful. However, Christ, that he might give us this salvation of body and spirit, suffered a cruel manhandling and death. Christ suffered to redeem mankind. He was rejected, ridiculed and buffeted as a sacrifice for the redemption of mankind. Finally he died like a malefactor on the cross, in deep, excruciating but undeserved pain. Why? Because he taught and preached against the world. He challenged the powerful religious bigots and sinful rulers of his time who worshipped God in error and sin. They were determined to silence him by any means possible. For three and half years God did not allow them to silence Jesus. They opposed and lied about him but the multitude still followed him. When the message of the gospel had penetrated and was grasped by faithful messengers, God opened the door for Jesus to pay the ultimate price through a cruel death. He shed his own blood for sin. The apostles of Jesus and all preachers of the gospel were to spread the same message Jesus preached. This message which excited the anger of the devil when Jesus preached would excite the same anger of the devil when preached by the apostles and disciples of Jesus. Therefore these preachers of truth would also not escape the same fate of suffering as endured by their master. The devil cannot entertain the preaching of the gospel in spirit and truth as this in fact means preaching against him. He will therefore ensure that the preaching of the gospel is disrupted and also that the preachers are made to suffer in various ways. After the ascension of Jesus and the descent of the Holy Ghost the apostles and disciples of Jesus preached with the same courage and truthfulness of the Lord Jesus. This provoked the devil and through the hands of rulers and influential men and women, the apostles died cruel deaths. They refused to recant of their faith and sealed their faith with their blood. They suffered for doing the work of Christ and for refusing to compromise with sin in all its shape and form. After the apostles, innocent blood of saints continued to flow as they were killed by rulers of this world and sometimes at the hands of their fellow backslidden Christian associates. Up to this day there are still regions of the world where Christians are still suffering persecution for their faith. However, in the civilised world, human rights laws have been enacted to protect all citizens including Christians from persecution by the anti-Christian society in which they live. Seeing this, the devil has also devised counter measures to ensure a permanent disruption of the preaching of the Gospel of Christ and suffering of saints. Churches themselves have become a source of controversy, unending misunderstanding and splits. This is mainly born out of corruption, power struggles and deception, traits which the church should be preaching against. The church is supposed to be the best example of what unity is on earth. But if the source becomes the best example of that disunity trait then everything falls apart. The reason there is so many denominations sprouting up is because of interpretations of the scriptures to suite the preacher's condition. There many undebatable teachings of the Bible which are now being accepted in many churches. One of the best examples is no divorce and remarriage but a number of church groups accept it because their leader has failed on this. Christ is one, the bible is one and the Holy Spirit is one and there is no disunity in all three. They agree. How is it possible for those who say they have Christ and the Holy Ghost to disagree? The answer to this is that it is the smart warfare of the devil against the preaching of the gospel of Christ. So many variations means so many errors and no error can save mankind. There is actually more spiritual death through Christian misunderstandings than when there was direct persecution. Therefore the actual suffering of Christians continues with intensity even if no shed blood is visible. Christian men and women must gird themselves for this kind of modern and smart warfare and be prepared to resist it. Daily vigilantes against workers of iniquity especially in church will preserve the truth of Christ. According to the Bible there will be proliferation of apostasy in churches in the last days. There is no reason to doubt this from what we witness in our age and the Word of God is infallible. *Refer to (2 Timothy 3:1-5; Matthew 24).*

CHAPTER 8

THE EARTHLY WALK

Beloved, now are we the sons of God, and it doth not yet appear what we shall be: but we know that, when he shall appear, we shall be like him; for we shall see him as he is. And every man that hath this hope in him purifieth himself, even as he is pure, (1 John 3:1-3)

Since creation, man was meant to live in society. In so doing they have to associate with other people, some as relatives, workmates or friends or even enemies. All these people have a degree of influence on the way that one conducts his or her life. The affinity that binds these people together is born out of some common interest. Relatives are bound by blood, workmates by the need for each individual to fend for self and friends by mutual affection and so on. Christianity is a way of life therefore it is also subject to the influence of the surroundings within which it is conducted as it is also supposed to influence the surroundings in which it is proclaimed. This is a matter which can make or unmake a Christian. It is of paramount importance that a Christian in all his or her activities of life chose friends of like interests and goals. The goal or objective of a Christian is to be righteous and to lead a blameless and holy life and at the end to enter heaven. This objective is then the separating screen which Christians will use in the selection of friends, wife or husband. They will need to have someone near who will encourage them towards the same goals rather than be a distraction. No association or position whatsoever will they allow interfering with their relationship to God. They realise and understand that the profession to which they have been called to be holy. Realising this and with this hope in heart and mind they strive to purify themselves and be like Jesus who shall host them in heaven. They want to be assured of membership to the church of God in heaven and citizenship of the new heaven and earth in which no evil will ever find way. A Christian therefore has nothing permanent on Earth to stick their hopes to.

Love:

Christians are God's children begotten through faith in the sin-cleansing blood of Jesus Christ *(1 Peter 1:23)*. Their deeds and way of life, which are completely at variance with worldliness, testify of their being children of God. They believe the Bible to be the Word of God. It is therefore their guiding principle compass and charter in all they do. As sons and daughters of God they have love for God and for mankind as their foremost task which they endeavour to fulfil in their life time. They understand that their profession is of love as the Lord Jesus summarised godliness and said, *"Jesus said unto him, Thou shalt love the Lord thy God with all thy heart, and with all thy soul, and with all thy mind. This is the first and great commandment. And the second is like unto it, Thou shalt love thy neighbour as thyself. On these two commandments hang all the law and the prophets." (Matthew 22:37-40).* To be a Christian therefore carries with it a great responsibility to both God and mankind. In the walk of life Christians have to show themselves that they love God through patience, longsuffering, charity, righteousness, temperance and the ability to uphold the truth under any circumstances. If the truth would make them loose an argument they would stick to it in order to please God and uphold the sanctity of godliness. Christians are that breed of people who spend a lot of time questioning themselves before acting on anything to ensure that their next action will be in line with the will of God. They will not act to please other people or to satisfy their own ambitions unless the actions are in line with the will of God. They are prisoners to the will of God. In order to please God a Christian strictly abides by the laws of the state in which he or she is resident. They can therefore not be found in any form of fraud or misleading information in order to obtain some benefit from the state or organisation in which they work. In the process of pleasing God a Christian does not need an earthly policeman to monitor them since the laws of God which bind them are by far more superior to the laws of any government on earth. They are monitored by their obedience to God whom they love with their hearts, soul and mind. It is only when the laws of the land start to push them towards disobedience to God that they will begin to question and if necessary disobey, because their motive is to please God not men. If in the process of pleasing God men are pleased then it is a Hallelujah and Amen! Christian are God's sons and daughters disguised by the flesh. Because they are still within this veil of the flesh the world will never really understand what a Christian stands for. Their strict way of life can be wrongly interpreted as passiveness and anti-social. Yet the reality is a Christian lives in unshakeable state of faith that when Jesus shall appear the second time they shall be like him and shall abide with him forever.

A Christian loves all people both sinners and none sinners. It is a law of God and the greatest show of love as demonstrated by Jesus himself who died for us sinners. His death was a substitute for our death. *"Greater love hath no man than this, that a man lay down his life for his friends" (John 15:13)*. During his time on earth, Jesus kept himself clean from all filthiness of the flesh. His main place of socialisation was the synagogues, hospices and homes of those that needed spiritual and physical healing. He befriended sinners not in sin but to inform them on how to come out of sin. He demonstrated what love for mankind is. Whenever need arose he gave to the hungry and poor. He did it for love not gain.

For healing, works of charity and preaching the Gospel of hope people followed him. None was ever coerced or threatened. He therefore who has hope to be one day with Christ and be like Christ has to put on these characteristics of the Lord. They have to cleanse themselves of all filthiness and questionable characteristics. Their true love for God and men is demonstrated by their way of life. Their homes are a paradise of piece to be emulated and admired by neighbours and relatives. Their church congregations are a demonstration of unity, godliness and love. They are an admiration of the world, as each member avoids scrutinising the failures of their fellow members but scrutinize their own shortcomings. If, perchance there is a disagreement amongst them, they through their love for God and their neighbours wlll solve the problem ensuring that at the end no member of the church of God or society will be negatively affected by their actions. They ensure that they are never the source of the condemnation of the name of God. This is the type of people who can never disagree to the point of consulting the human courts for adjudication *(1 Corinthians 6:1-3; Matthew 18:15-17).* They know that such action will destroy what they proclaim to be. They are prepared to lose all instead of being paraded in front of those they are meant to preach godliness to. They can indeed be taken to court by none Christians for any perceived wrong but not amongst themselves. If that happens is means either one or both of them do not have Christ controlling their lives. They are the type of people who strive to cleanse themselves and each one will remove whatever pride they may have for the sake of Christ. They remember the parable of the lost sheep when the shepherd left ninety nine to look for one lost one. Therefore they cannot afford to carelessly behave in any way that will result in any single soul doubting God *(Luke 15:4-7).* They endeavour to be like Jesus our Lord who sacrificed all majesty for us sinners. They remember how Jesus substituted for Barabbas the murderer. They live to show the light of Christ not through words but action. They are the salt and light of the world, who, when the world is at its worst of sin they demonstrate the best of love and righteousness.

Principled:

"Be ye not unequally yoked together with unbelievers: for what fellowship hath righteousness with unrighteousness? And what communion hath light with darkness? And what concord hath Christ with Belial? Or what part hath he that believeth with an infidel? And what agreement hath the temple of God with idols? For ye are the temple of the living God; ....Wherefore come out from among them, and be ye separate, saith the Lord, and touch not the unclean thing; and I will receive you." (2 Corinthians 6: 14-17).

Any meaningful profession is known for its principles and values. These principles and values are the ones which differentiate it from the other professions. Christianity as we have seen has love, righteousness, piece, unity, holiness, patience, temperance as some of its values. Any true and serious Christian will be found to possess these characteristics regardless of which denomination they may apportion themselves to. As long they are born of God they cannot be otherwise. The saved will be known for their good works just like the unsaved will also be known of their ungodly works. It is God's desire that Christians should love sinners but it is not his desire that they should have intimate relationships with them. The act of salvation changes the behaviour, interests and objectives of the saved. If, as an example, a person was a womaniser before being saved, the power of salvation will completely cleanse him from this type of sin. It therefore does not make sense to see this person always in the company of women as before. His acquired righteousness now has no part or agreement with those in darkness of sin to still make them friends because their interests collide. This goes for all other vices practiced by mankind before they are saved. A Christian will have no part in these endless practices and sports of the world. They cannot be found in fraud, gambling, drinking, smoking, gossip, backbiting, lying and many other practices of the unsaved world. They cleanse themselves as he (Jesus) is clean. Christian come from a diverse number of cultures, religion and idol worship. Some of these cultures and religions involve some inhuman practices, rituals and sacrifices which are at complete variance with righteousness. True Christians built on the foundation which is Christ will separate themselves from these. At times this separation may cause resentment, anger and hatred from relatives and friends but a Christian should not worry about that. They should stand by their principle of abstinence from all appearance of evil in obedience to the word of God, knowing that it is better to please God than mankind. It can also be dangerous to knowingly disobey the will of God like what Ananias and Sapphire did, which resulted in instant punishment from God.

True Christians are not fanatics but principled and reasonable men and women of God. The boundary of their lives is the Word of God and nothing more or less. If it becomes more then it is fanatic and if less it is hypocrisy. A Christian tours the narrow path of the word of God as his word rightly said, *"Because strait is the gate, and narrow is the way, which leadeth unto life, and few there be that find it." (Matthew 7:14)*. The pleasing of people is therefore not part of the Christian's agenda regardless of whether there is gain or loss. If it is to please mankind against God then for a Christian the result will always be a loss in order to win Christ. There is only one way to life and it is the way of holiness and the unclean cannot walk therein *(see Isaiah 35:8)*.

Whilst a Christian cares heartily for the spiritual and physical lives of mankind, his or her first duty is to ensure that they are first secured in Christ themselves by not indulging in any form of unrighteous act or deed. The Word says come out of them *(verse 17)*. It is a principle of living. Indeed to live a separated, solitary-like life can appear odd in society. However, the Lord Jesus says it is narrow way and if one once finds and remains in it, they have to oblige to its dictates. This is why few find it. This is a way which knows no compromise with sin and worldliness. For this reason Christians have suffered loss of many things preferring to lose than to fight in preservation of their cherished status in Christ.

In a world full of cheating and divorces, Christian men will love their wives as Christian women reverence their husbands, being drawn together by their fear and love for God. They are children of light and will live to show light to the world full of sin. Men will no longer treat their wives as second-class citizens of the earth but fellow citizens, partners and a help meet for them as the bible says. Wife beating, subjugation and suppression will therefore be anathema amongst the children of light. The harassment of husbands by the contentious and brawling women will cease as Christ takes control of their hearts. Home becomes a paradise and a place of harmony and peace. The husband and the wife will complement each other in the home and the truth of Christianity will be visible to neighbours, relatives and friends.

Family Care:

"But if any provide not for his own, and especially for those of his own house, he hath denied the faith, and is worse than an infidel" (1 Timothy 5:8)

In most cases God blesses Christians with wives, husbands, children, relatives and friends. This blessing carries with it some serious responsibility assigned by God, first to the family and then to the wider world. Faith in God is practical. *"It is the evidence of things not seen" (Hebrews 11:1).* When God instructs us to do something we oblige because we have full trust that what he has said will come to pass. That way we turn faith into practice. Therefore if a Christian has a family they are duty bound to provide for them in direct obedience to the word of God. They are to ensure that they have food, shelter, clothing and education. If there is a will, God will always provide extra to those who work honestly with their own hands in obedience to the word of God to provide for their families? Indeed, in most cases they can never be rich but God will assist them to get just enough to provide for the family's needs. God never instructs something to be done and fail to provide the means. The act of providing for families is not a preserve for Christians only. It is natural that parents want to provide for their families regardless of religion or no religion. However due to the power of darkness which befalls many in the world, they regrettably end up failing to fulfil this instinct. To a Christian, however it is not optional as they risk being worse than those who refuse or care less to worship God. These are what are referred to as infidels in scripture. A Christian should not be worse than a sinner otherwise they will not be fit to preach or testify to them of a redeeming Christ. Christians preach Christ effectively through their practical and exemplary ways of living. People are not looking for church groups which are so plenty, they are looking for a righteous way of living. This is only found in Christ.

If a Christian does a lot of charity works in society whilst neglecting his own family or house, he or she is going against the will of God. The first task in the works of charity is to ensure that our own families are provided for in terms of all the basic requirements of life and not in extravagant living and fashion. It is ungodly to have children and then fail to provide them even with the excuse that one is engaged in the work of God. God cannot contradict himself what he says he fulfills. God has never neglected his own children. He caters for them spiritually, materially and physically on a daily basis. When Israel travelled from Egypt to Canaan God made sure that Moses was there to lead them and provide them with all spiritual food, he also provided them with food for the flesh and catered for their health *(Exodus 15:26)*. In the Christian era God is still the same. He provides his own with what they deserve and ensures their health whilst he will be there to heal them whenever it becomes necessary.

The act of providing for the family binds the husband to the wife and to their children. Neglect of the family for any reason, including working for God drives a dangerous wedge in the family. It drives children away from God as they see him as the reason of their suffering. As the Christian's children, are God's people he expects them to worship him. To do something that separates them from God is the work of the devil. Those who are full time workers of God must take heed of this important admonition. Any so called work of God done to drive the flock to the devil becomes the work of Satan. The first law which carries a blessing is about the care and honor of our parents *(Exodus 20:12)*. A Christian should therefore ensure as much as possible to look after the parents as their central family. This is true godliness and neglect of parents an abomination.

"As we have therefore opportunity, let us do good unto all men, especially unto them who are of the household of faith", *(Galatian 6: 10)*. Once we have fulfilled the basic needs of our families we can then look to help our brothers and sisters, relatives, other Christians and the wider world. God always bless the generous with more as he cannot be out given by mankind.

The Dress question

"Go ye therefore into the highways, and as many as ye shall find, bid to the marriage. So those servants went out into the highways, and gathered together all as many as they found, both bad and good: and the wedding was furnished with guests; And when the king came in to see the guests, he saw there a man which had not on a wedding garment: And he saith unto him, Friend, how camest thou in hither not having a wedding garment? And he was speechless. Then said the king to the servants, Bind him hand and foot, and take him away, and cast him into outer darkness, there shall be weeping and gnashing of teeth. For many are called, but few are chosen." (Matthew 22:9-

Salvation is the mortification of the old nature to put on the new life in Christ Jesus. Old things pass away and all become new because a new man or woman in Christ is renewed in the knowledge of God who has re-created him or her. This is a total revolution or change in the life of any who is born of God. The mind and knowledge of those who have been saved is towards being a living image of the unseen God who influences their spiritual lives and hence has power to control the passions of their flesh too. They have put off the old man or woman with all his or her deeds. It is to be emphasised that all the deeds of the old nature are put off including all forms of sin, associations, sport, styles be they hair or dress. There is a way that the old nature wants to present itself to the world and there is a way that the new nature wants to present itself to the world too. Dressing is one way that mankind present themselves. The way that one dresses oneself tells a quick story about who they are even before an introduction is made, unless they are impostors. It should therefore be correct to say the way the old nature dresses before Christ come into the life of a person must be at variance with the way the new nature would want to dress because they are influenced by completely different attractions, interest and desires. It would therefore be wrong to conclude this book without addressing the issue of dressing as related to those built on the true foundation of godliness upon which no gates of hell can prevail. Can the unworldly continue to dress in the same manner as the worldly? Can the new man continue to dress as the old man? The answer must be an empathic no!

Jesus once taught about the importance of the wedding garment at a wedding. The invitation was first extended to the relatives and friends of the bride and groom. However the invitation to the wedding became open to everybody because those who were invited for the wedding had just ignored the invitation for their own other commitments. Although the invitation had become open the conditions to enter the wedding hall remained the same. All who would partake in the wedding had to put on a wedding garment. This was the special dress for the occasion which would differentiate those taking part in the ceremony and those not taking part. As is always the case someone or maybe more thought it unfair for the Master of the ceremony to impose those restrictions, instead they wanted to take part per their own conditions and therefore forced themselves to the wedding hall without the differentiating attire. When the master of the ceremony came, his first task was to ensure that only people with the correct attire were taking part in the wedding. Those who were without the garment were to be removed and cast out. It seems that actually those without the wedding garment were the majority in the hall for the word finally says, *"For many are called, but few are chosen,"* meaning that at last those who took part in the wedding or the chosen ones were just but a few. These were the obedient, humble, sober and properly dressed guests, apt to do the will of the King of the ceremony. The master of the ceremony was satisfied with the few but properly dressed wedding guests.

It does not matter how controversial the dress question might be amongst the Christian world, it remains an important factor which preaches of either the new nature or old nature of that dressed individual. A Christian man or woman cannot accept a situation where, through their dressing, they get associated with sin. They will desire an identity which lifts up their profession, as they are built on a sure foundation of righteousness and holiness which they are not ashamed of. Paul says, *"For I am not ashamed of the gospel of Christ: for it is the power of God unto salvation to everyone that believeth; to the Jew first, and also to the Greek" (Romans 1:16).* Being decently and modestly dressed is a characteristic of the sobriety of those built on the sure foundation of godliness. I do not mean to judge those in their own professions or the world. That is none of my business. But for a professing Christian, a man and woman of God who preaches the holiness of God, what has mini-skirts to do with their profession. Indeed, what has exposing dressing to do with a man or woman of God? What benefit and standing in society does a breeches bestow on a man of God? Does it edify at all for mothers and their girl children to leave their houses and go into society and expose their bodies to the world in the name of fashion. Yes indeed for those who have not known Christ, it does not matter for that is who they are, but for the redeemed of God it should matter. Those who proffer godliness should in all things including dressing act as becomes their profession. The redeemed should realise that they are on a wedding roll call all the time. They clothe for their bridegroom Christ and are not ashamed of it because to live for Christ is to live for eternity to them. The redeemed, those founded on the incorruptible foundation which is Jesus the WORD of God should clothe as if they are waiting for transport to take them to heaven. Their destination is the paradise of God.

The bible is specific about women's way of clothing. However it does not mean that men must be carelessly and worldly dressed. All Christians must therefore ensure what they wear meets the merits of their profession and avoid not to follow the attention seeking spirit of the worldly. *"In like manner also, that women adorn themselves in modest apparel, with shamefacedness and sobriety" (Timothy 2: 9a)*. Modest means humble, low-key and free of vanity. Again it must be emphasised that the dressing must be modest not fanatic so as to preserve the dignity of the person. It should be the desire of a Christian to be staid and bashful and not to be the one going around drawing the attention of the world to oneself through some flashy, Vanity Fair kind of dressing and make-ups. A Christian built on the foundation which is Jesus will always want the attention to be given to Jesus. John Baptist said of Jesus, *"He must increase, but I must decrease." (John 3:30)*.

The Hair and Head:

"Ye are our epistle written in our hearts, known and read of all men: Forasmuch as ye are manifestly declared to be the epistle of Christ ministered by us, written not with ink, but with the Spirit of the living God; not in tables of stone, but in fleshy tables of the heart" (2 Corinthians 3:2-3).

The strength of the teachings of the apostles and indeed of all true teachers and preachers of the Gospel of Christ could never be acknowledged by their word of mouth, but through its ability to change the lives of men and women. The righteous and holy lives of Christians preach the Gospel to the world better than any preacher can do. Men can doubt what we say but not what we are and what we do. To God the external man is as important as the internal for there are no contradictions with him. One cannot claim to be a Christian whilst their life goes contrary to the teaching of the Gospel. The statutes and God's laws are engraved on the heart of the saved in order to control both the internal and external life. People know Christ from the external life of Christians for that is what they see. It must be graciously and lovingly at total variance and conflict to the world.

For this reason the word of God also deals with how a Christian man and woman should treat even the hair of their head. There should be a difference between the hair style of the worldly and that of the Godly in accordance with the word of God. It is not man's dictation but God's statute.

We are living in a world which is subdued of the devil and in our time the words of the Bible have become relevant to all mankind even those which in time past it seemed to segregate. Today both men and women spend a substantial amount of their incomes and time working on their hair, plaiting and braiding it. To women they seek to increase beauty and attractiveness and to men it is mostly carnal confusion. Some will contest this statement but I find no other reason for those activities, other than the foregoing. They cheat daily those who are attracted by vanity. For this reason, the Bible is specific about this kind of behaviour: *"Whose adorning let it not be that outward adorning of plaiting the hair..." (1 Pet 3:2).* Women who stand and live for Christ should not find this difficult to practice as their aim is to please God. It is true vanity for someone to go to the supermarket to buy other people's hair in order to try and beautify the self. For the word of God to emphasise so deeply about the hair of a woman means that this problem mostly centres on ladies. Instead of spending time and money on the corruptible hair which needs to be changed and redone daily they should put on Christ, wearing decent clothing and a properly covered head according to the word of God. I believe women should simply ensure care of their natural hair and avoid plaiting and braiding as this just contradicts all what the word of God says.

This subject of hair plaiting is not for the ordinary women and men. They will not understand it or believe it due to their carnal mind. It is for the redeemed. The bible goes deeper and says:

"But every woman that prayeth or prophesieth with her head uncovered dishonoureth her head: for that is even all one as if she were shaven; for if the woman be not covered, let her also be shorn: but if it be a shame for a woman to be shorn or shaven, let her be covered. For a man indeed ought not to cover his head, forasmuch as he is the image and glory of God: but the woman is the glory of the man. For the man is not of the woman: but the woman of the man. Neither was the man created for the woman; but the woman for the man. For this cause ought the woman to have power on her head because of the angels. Nevertheless neither is the man without the woman, neither the woman without the man, in the Lord. For as the woman is of the man, even so is the man also by the woman; but all things of God. Judge in yourselves: is it comely that a woman pray unto God uncovered? Doth not even nature

itself teach you, that, if a man have long hair, it is a shame unto him? But if a woman have long hair, it is a glory to her: for her hair is given her for a covering. But if any man seem to be contentious, we have no such custom, neither the churches of God"(1 Corinthians 11:5-15).

There is really no need for a woman of God to plait or braid the hair because, at last, they need to cover it. By virtue of nature woman have long hair and do not grow bald head. Hair is a woman's glory. Not artificially attached hair but her own, God-given hair is a glory to her, given to keep her covered. But God wants this natural, long and well looked-after hair of a woman to be covered as well. Not the face and head, but the head only that is the area where hair grows. God does not want exaggerations either way. If a woman thinks she must not cover her head then she must shave her head. However if she shaves her head, she becomes a shameful woman. Therefore those Christian women out to serve the Lord will keep their her clean, long and well looked after and on top of it fix a fitting and clean head covering. Whilst this is contestable amongst the worldly women it cannot be for the Christian women who rely for their instruction and guidance on the word of God. Also the Christian men of God cannot put on long hair. It is an abomination and a shame to do so as the scriptures say. There are indeed some religious cults which refer to the dread locks of Samson and the vow of a Nazarene. These men stand to be reminded that Paul himself was a Nazarene who strongly advocated through the spirit of God that it is shameful for a man to have long hair. A Christian is someone permanently separated from sin and does not need the periods of separation which were symbolised by long and uncombed hair during the period of the law. Grace has made us free from all these rituals. Christian men have therefore to maintain a standard short and well looked after haircut together with a clean shaven face which depicts their unique and smart profession, *"Ye are our epistle written in our hearts, known and read of all men."*

Flee Worldliness:

"Love not the world, neither the things that are in the world. If any man love the world, the love of the Father is not in him. For all that is in the world, the lust of the flesh, and the lust of the eyes, and the pride of life, is not of the Father, but is of the world" (1 John 2: 15-16).

The scripture above warns of what has become the bane of Christianity of our time. The reformation was a direct product of Christianity inclined to worldliness by the Catholics which the reformers disagreed with. Whilst the Catholics have not changed their practices, they have recently been joined by a more cunning and zealous group of religious zealots pretending to preach Christ whilst amassing pleasure and wealth for themselves. These so called prophets and preachers of the word of God are in fact preachers of wealth and prosperity sprouting from divers' places in the world and have confused the vulnerable, unsuspecting and unschooled penitents who otherwise will be seeking God with a meaningful heart. They have also given foothold to the anti-Christ who now uses this wickedness for his own evil ends and attacks against Christ.

Jesus is the best example of what Christianity should be. He, being God and therefore very rich, demonstrated humility, simplicity and the spirit to share whilst he was on Earth. The spirit to cater and care for orphans and widows, the disabled and neglected. But today the rebuked and despised spirit of Dives has taken control of many church leaders and their trusted lieutenants. A situation which exists where ministers of religion find themselves driving the latest, very expensive cars, living in posh suburbs and houses and wearing designer clothing whilst their congregates live in squalor is very ungodly and anti-word of God, anti-Christ and a true example of extreme lust of the eyes and pride of life. The word of God gives a clear warning about this sin saying, *"dearly beloved, I beseech you as strangers and pilgrims, abstain from fleshly lusts, which war against the soul..." (1 Pet 2:11).* Why should a man of God who knows and preaches the truth that he and his fellow Christians are but pilgrims and strangers on Earth want to possess several high-class cars and houses amongst a suffering and hungry society, unless he or she has lost the vision along the way and considers this Earth a permanent home. Men and women of old who held sacred the old-time religion of Christ did not build strong houses on earth but chose to share the earthly riches with their fellow, less privileged brothers and sisters and to live in simple houses whilst they strived to live righteously and one day be ushered into the new Jerusalem in the heaven of God.

The fleshly lust is brewed from within the heart and thereby wreaks havoc to all what is called Christianity resulting in a very corrupted man or woman instead of a Christian. Many deadly corrupt practices are reported in the media today ranging from rapes, adultery, fornication, thefts and forgeries committed by priests, bishops and church leaders. This shows the loss of focus by the professors of Christianity. Instead of abstinence they join hands in the practice of sin. These are the true last days prophesied in the bible and those Christians with the Spirit of God should be awake to quickly recognize this marauding spirit of the devil and resist it. *"This know also, that in the last days perilous times shall come. For men shall be lovers of their own selves ... lovers of pleasures more than lovers of God" 2 Timothy 3:1-4.*

Here I am not at all advocating for poverty in church (which is already rampant anywhere in and out of church) but that the ministers and their reverends should live and practice the truth of the Bible which they preach and share the wealth derived from donations by the congregates with the poor in their churches. That would be true love. But I have known churches where congregational members eat food from the bin thrown there by fellow Christians whilst they are gathering for the so-called camp meetings and conventions. In the meantime the reverends and their trustees will be feasting with their families. The gap between the theory being preached in the sermons and the practice

95

is like the North and South Poles of the earth. The real demise of Christianity is born out of this kind of behaviour by the clergy. Christ was a servant of the people to the tune of wiping the disciples' feet himself. But the reverends of this world want the congregants to brush their feet. They are masters and lords and not shepherds of the flock of God.

The love of the world has drained and wrecked many Christians who started the walk well but later along the way entangled themselves with credits which they could not afford to pay back. They became despondent, discouraged and left the way. Many through uncontrolled closeness to women or men were overcome by fleshly last and ended up in adultery or fornication. A Christian should have boundaries and limits within which no compromise can be entertained.

Paul cautioned Timothy, the youthful minister to be wary and flee youthful lusts, for they can wreck and destroy good character, *"Flee also youthful lusts: but follow righteousness, faith, charity, peace, with them that call on the Lord out of a pure heart2", 2 Tim 2:22.*

Christianity means to follow righteousness, nothing more or less. Any slight compromise on righteousness is a failure and backsliding. There are many attractive and legal things being done by mankind which are anti-Christian. A good example is the lottery and the other is football. These things use the deceit in riches to lure the whole world to contribute for the enrichment of a few. Christians should be warned to keep away from these. Many families suffer whilst the gambling father or mother has lost all hard earned cash to the rich, because of the desire for riches. Football is indeed one of the major attractions of the 21st century. It has become a religion pulling many people from the worship of God on the Lord's Day. It is a real source of some of the deadly corrupt practices at the highest level of society. All that football is about is enriching the players and the sponsors at the expense of the poor. The Bible says, *"And the cares of this world, and the deceitfulness of riches, and the lusts of other* things entering in, choke the word, and it becometh unfruit-ful (Mark 4:19). The seeking of riches and lusts of the eyes when entertained will choke the word in the heart and it will cease to desire the deeper things of God and subsequently it withers and dies.

God looks after his own and this is a true saying. There is, therefore no need for one to strenuously seek riches and even position to the point of sacrificing so dear a salvation. All good things come from the Lord. For something earthly a Christian should never fight to the end but for the heaven of God. If God destines someone for a certain task on earth men can fight him or her but God's plan will not fail. Moses is our best example of a man chosen by God but rejected of man. At the end God's plan triumphed 40 years later. It is true those who fought him thought they had triumphed see-ing the passage of time but they achieved nothing, died and were buried by Egyptians whilst Moses was buried by angels Jude 9. Never use deceit for any form of gain for *"the eye of the Lord is upon them that fear him……..."* and to fear God is to depart from evil.

Conclusion:

"And I said unto him, Sir, thou knowest. And he said to me, These are they which came out of great tribulation, and have washed their robes, and made them white in the blood of the Lamb. Therefore are they before the throne of God, and serve him day and night in his temple: and he that sitteth on the throne shall dwell among them. They shall hunger no more, neither thirst anymore; neither shall the sun light on them, nor any heat. For the Lamb which is in the midst of the throne shall feed them, and shall lead them unto living fountains of waters: and God shall wipe away all tears from their eyes." (Revelation 7:14-17).

Amen!

Lightning Source UK Ltd.
Milton Keynes UK
UKOW04f2017280815

257747UK00004B/138/P